SUCCESSFUL PRESENTATION SKILLS

Better Management Skills

This highly popular range of inexpensive paperbacks covers all areas of basic management. Practical, easy to read and instantly accessible, these guides will help managers to improve their business or communication skills. Those marked * are available on audio cassette.

The books in this series can be tailored to specific company requirements. For further details, please contact the publisher, Kogan Page, telephone 0171 278 0433, fax 0171 837 6348.

Be a Successful Supervisor
Be Positive
Building High Performance Teams
Business Creativity
Business Ethics
Business Etiquette
Consult Your Customers
Creating a Learning Organisation
Creative Decision-making
Creative Thinking in Business
Delegating for Results
Effective Employee Participation
Effective Meeting Skills
Effective Performance Appraisals*
Effective Presentation Skills
First Time Supervisor
Get Organised!
Goals and Goal Setting
How to Communicate Effectively*
How to Develop a Positive
  Attitude*
How to Develop Assertiveness
How to Motivate People*
How to Understand Financial
  Statements

How to Write a Staff Manual
Improving Employee Performance
Improving Relations at Work
Keeping Customers for Life
Make Every Minute Count*
Managing Organisational
  Change
Managing Part-Time Employees
Managing Quality Customer
  Service
Managing Your Boss
Marketing for Success
Memory Skills in Business
Mentoring
NLP for Business Success
Office Management
Productive Planning
Project Management
Quality Customer Service
Rate Your Skills as a Manager
Self-managing Teams
Selling Professionally
Successful Telephone Techniques
Systematic Problem-solving
Team Building

SUCCESSFUL PRESENTATION SKILLS

Producing and Delivering Top Quality Presentations

Andrew Bradbury

KOGAN PAGE

For Dave and Caroline
In return for their gift of hope

First published in 1995
Reprinted 1997 (twice)

Kogan Page Limited
120 Pentonville Road
London N1 9JN

© Andrew J Bradbury 1995

British Library Cataloguing in Publication Data

A CIP record for this book is available from the British Library.

ISBN 0-7494-1749-8

Typeset by BookEns Ltd, Royston, Herts.
Printed and bound in Great Britain by Clays Ltd, St. Ives plc.

Contents

CHAPTER 1
Where Do You Want to Go?

Do *you* need this book?

How important is it for you and your company that your presentations should be top quality, memorable and effective? Do you stage your presentations as part of an overall strategy, or just whenever 'it seems like a good idea'?

A favourite business buzzword at the moment is 'differentiation' – the means of making your company more attractive to a potential customer than any other. In practice, the only way you can really differentiate your company is by making the most effective sales pitch – the most impressive presentation. Yet if many of the presentations I've seen over the years are anything to go by, most of us – from junior salesperson to managing director – could derive significant benefits from a crash course in basic presentation skills. And that's just what this book is all about.

Most of the tens of thousands of presentations that are going on at any given moment during any working day are intended to sell a product or service, pass on information, elicit ideas, or introduce and develop new skills.

In short, if you *ever* have to deal with other people, in *any* kind of business situation, this book has something to offer.

All the world's a stage

Almost any kind of business transaction involves some degree of presentation skill. Guiding a new colleague through the basic office procedures, reporting back to a departmental meeting, or giving the members of the board an overview of a new project – in each situation you will be giving a presentation.

In the first case you may sit down with the new employee and chat over a few key features of the job, while in the second example you might jot down a few notes and even prepare a foil or two. For the presentation to the board you would probably take several days to prepare and rehearse your script, and to design OHP foils and handouts. Superficially, the three events may appear quite different, yet at heart they are all the same.

Alternatively, you may be visiting a prospective business partner, sitting round the kitchen table with a cup of coffee while you run through the facts and figures on an A4 pad. But is that really any different from discussing the same facts and figures with a dozen or so people, using a flipchart or a whiteboard instead of sheets of A4 paper?

The seven basic steps

This book is based on the assumption that the whole presentation process consists of seven basic steps:

1. Decide what you want to achieve.
2. Decide whether a formal presentation is the best way to achieve this objective.
3. If you decide to go ahead with the presentation, decide what form it should take.
4. Prepare a script (in whatever form suits you best).
5. Design and prepare your visual aids and handouts.
6. Rehearse.
7. Do it!

The only guaranteed way to produce a poor presentation is

through inadequate preparation. I've seen senior business people give the most appalling presentations – because they refused to learn a few basic skills.

The good news is that I've also seen presentations by people who had no special qualifications other than a willingness to put in the necessary time and effort. And many of those presentations were just great!

A good presentation is no more than effective communication between two or more human beings. There's no mystery to it – unless you've never had the opportunity to find out how to do it right. It is a skill, and like any other skill it can be learned. And the very fact that you are reading this book tells me that you are a person who is willing to learn.

As Chris Sullivan, a senior consultant with Guardian Business Services, explains:

> Even people who look unpromising can draw something out from within themselves. People who stutter and stammer will still stutter and stammer, but they can present effectively in spite of that.

Of course this book won't turn you into a Winston Churchill or John F Kennedy overnight. Those men, and other men and women like them, have all shared one quality that no book can give you – the *desire to communicate*. That's one quality only you can provide. It doesn't have to be a desire to speak to nations. You don't even have to plan to address rallies of several hundred people. You only have to want to make that basic contact with your audience, even though that audience is a man, a boy and a dog, as the saying goes.

Presentations are about communication

First and foremost, this book is about *communicating*. It will show you how to understand your audience, and how to relate to them in the most effective manner.

It assumes no prior knowledge, and covers everything you need to know to deliver successful presentations.

By the way, you might want to arm yourself with a pen or

highlighter to mark the points that are of special interest to you, points that you particularly want to remember.

Many people find that the very act of underlining or highlighting a piece of information helps them to absorb the information more readily. Maybe it would work for you, too?

CHAPTER 2
2, 4, 6, 8 – How Do You Communicate?

It's not what you say

One of the best kept secrets of the business world costs companies vast amounts of money, wastes millions of working hours per year and can be summed up in two short sentences:

Most business presentations do not achieve their intended purpose. Worse still, they frequently achieve *nothing* of any value!

Have you ever been in a situation where you felt that you had really presented a very convincing case for or against a certain course of action, yet nobody seemed to be the least bit affected by what you said?

This apparent failure may simply be due to the fact that you were saying something that nobody wanted to hear. It is much more likely, however, that you were placing too much dependence upon the power of your logic, and paying too little attention to other aspects of your very personal contribution to the presentation.

For example, when you are trying to influence other people, how aware are you of your body language, your vocal style and your 'presence' (that vague personal quality also known as 'charm' or 'charisma')? And do you realise that, where there are conflicting messages, the way that these factors are perceived by other people will normally far outweigh the effect of anything you might *say*, be it in an intimate conversation or in a major presentation?

Studies from both Britain and America show that we tend to base our judgement of other people on three main characteristics:

- Verbal Content = 7%
- Vocal Interest = 38%
- Body Language = 55%

While the exact percentages may vary slightly, depending on the particular situation, these figures show that at least 90 per cent of your public image depends on *how* you look and sound rather than *what* you actually say.

It's the way that you say it

Not only do we pay close attention to these 'non-verbal' signals, but it seems that we also have quite clear ideas as to what the signals mean. For example, how well do you know your own voice? Is it deep and gruff, about average or a little high pitched? Do you speak quickly, slowly or at a medium pace? Do you have an extensive range of tones and inflections which make your voice interesting to listen to, or (be honest) does your voice tend to become rather monotonous if you have to speak for any length of time (over five minutes' continuous speech, for example)?

The answer you give may explain a lot about the way that other people react to you. A person who speaks slowly and in a lower than average tone is widely perceived as being powerful and credible. Someone with a faster, higher toned voice will be seen as enthusiastic but lightweight through to positively untrustworthy.

And what about your body language? Here, too, you may be 'saying' a lot more about yourself without ever realising it.

For example, a person whose gestures are few and far between is seen as being powerful, deliberate and intelligent. The sort of person who makes frequent, expansive gestures may be seen as frivolous or even three sandwiches short of a picnic.

Remember, then, if your overall personal style is inconsistent, your audience will base their impressions on the 93 per cent non-verbal signals you put out rather than the 7 per cent of verbal content, no matter how clever, logical and reasonable that verbal content may be.

I'm really pleased to be here – maybe

Here's a simple example of how this might work in practice.

Imagine that you have been invited to attend the launch of a new product which the manufacturers hope will be a world-beater. After a rather long wait a door opens and a man enters and walks wearily to the podium set up at the front of the room. He is tall and well dressed in a dark suit, white shirt and discreetly patterned tie. His hair is carefully styled and his shoes look smart, well polished and expensive. He reaches the podium and waits for a minute or so with shoulders bowed, grasping the sides of the lectern as though his life depended on it. He stares down at his notes and *avoids* establishing eye contact with the audience as he makes his opening remarks in a voice that is tired and monotonous, even depressed:

> 'Good morning, ladies and gentlemen. May I start by saying how nice it is to see such a large audience. I think I can safely promise you a very interesting and stimulating day ...'

Do *you* believe that he is pleased to see you? Do *you* believe his promise that the events which are to follow will be interesting and stimulating? Are you looking forward to what is to come – or working out your chances of getting a refund if you leave straightaway?

I suspect that your answers would reflect a very low level of expectation. Yet this cannot be due to anything that has been said. If you take the words out of context, the message they convey is polite, positive, even enthusiastic. But once the verbal content is combined with contradictory vocal and body language signals, it is the signals which we believe, not the verbal content.

No matter what the situation, if your *style* of presentation isn't an audience grabber, the *content* begins to become irrelevant. At the worst extreme, a truly unskilled presenter can put material across in such a way that the members of the audience not only don't take it in, they don't even care that they haven't taken it in. They're just glad when the presentation is over.

In short, the most brilliant speech ever written will ultimately depend for its success on the *presentation style* of the speech maker, and not on the contents of the speech itself.

One of the best known examples of this phenomenon at work must be the pre-election debate between John F Kennedy and Richard M Nixon when the two men were competing for the post of President of the United States in 1960.

Those people who only *heard* the debate on radio had to rely on the verbal content and vocal signals to guide their perceptions. Most people in this group regarded Nixon as the better candidate.

Of the people who *saw* the debate on television, and received verbal content and the vocal signals and saw the body language of the two speakers, the majority perceived John F Kennedy as being a far more credible candidate.

It is a simple fact of history that it was Nixon who had the policies, but Kennedy who won the presidency!

The presenter who can create rapport with her audience is operating on both the conscious and the subconscious levels. At its best the effect can be quite magical. The good news is that there is nothing 'magical' about it. It is a skill which almost anyone can master with a little time and effort.

CHAPTER 3
When You Feel the Fear ...

Panic now – and avoid the rush

You're sitting quietly at your desk when suddenly the call comes: 'We need a presentation, and only *you* can do it!' What do you feel? Pride? Caution? Or unadulterated

PANIC

If you opted for panic, why not use this as a five-part reminder of the key elements of a good presentation:

Outline your **P**urpose
Analyse your **A**udience
Identify the **N**eed
Collate your **I**nformation
Prepare your **C**ommunication

Purpose
In many cases the purpose of a presentation will not be a matter of choice but will be dictated for you by someone else, or by the context in which the presentation will take place:

- Your department head asks you to show Sid Gorringe (a new employee) the ropes.
- You are chosen to give senior management a brief overview of the work done by your team.
- It is your task to round out the proceedings at a meeting of the sales team in a positive and motivating fashion.

But beware of taking too much for granted. Make sure that you have a clear idea of what the presentation is about. If necessary, push for further information until you are sure that you have a precise understanding of that purpose:

- Are you required to train Sid Gorringe in some specific tasks, or simply familiarise him with the general routine?
- Are you doing a solo presentation to senior management, or are you one of half a dozen speakers?
- What are the current sales figures like? Will your own presentation be preceded by rewards or recriminations?

There's many a good presentation which has fallen by the wayside because the speaker wasn't clear about his purpose.

Audience
In the examples we've just looked at, a specific audience has been mentioned – the new employee, senior management, and the sales team.

Always find out as much as you can about your intended audience, and focus your presentation accordingly.

Need
Every presentation has a *reason*, and *needs*. The *purpose* of taking Sid Gorringe through the office procedures may be to get him up to speed as quickly as possible, but what are his *needs*? Does he need detailed instructions, or a brief refresher? What do you need to be able to meet this requirement? Can you 'do it with your eyes shut'? Or do you need to do some research? Is this a routine situation, or a possible step up the ladder?

The more clearly you can define the *needs* of the situation, the more chance you have of giving a really 'spot on' presentation.

Information
So, now you know who your presentation is for, and why. But what information should be included to achieve the required outcome? Give out too little information, and the event

becomes a waste of everyone's time. Give too much information and most of it will be forgotten by the next day – and the event becomes a waste of everyone's time.

The more accurately you define your goal, the easier it will be to determine what must go into the presentation – and what can be left out.

Communication

What visual aids will you use (if any)? Where will the event be staged? What kind of follow-up will be required?

This is the point at which you plan the structure of your presentation and consider the all-important question: How will it be perceived by your audience (will they hear what you *meant* to say, what you *did* say, or what they *think* you said)?

Your 'performing edge'

It is quite normal to feel some degree of apprehension when you are about to embark on an activity that is both important and, to a certain extent, unknown. Will the audience be responsive? Will your presentation meet their needs? Will the main power supply flow smoothly? A presenter who does not feel apprehension before an event is generally, in my experience, not nearly as skilled in delivering presentations as he thinks he is.

The 'secret' remedy for so-called stage fright is simply to acknowledge the feeling without letting it upset you. Trying to ignore the feeling is self-defeating – you have to keep thinking about it in order to remember what you are trying to ignore!

When you feel a little nervous, 'reframe' that feeling. Re-interpret what is happening to you as a process of revving up for a really successful performance. Remind yourself that a little extra adrenalin helps to give you a performing edge. Then concentrate on all the things that you are going to do to make this your best presentation yet.

Winning ways

A genuinely effective way to acquire new skills is to find out what acknowledged experts do, understand what makes them so successful, and then apply that behaviour in your own activities and thereby learn to duplicate that success.

Amway, the doyen of the network marketing companies, has seen its profits soar over the last few years, through the application of this technique. Amway distributors have duplicated excellence so successfully over the years that from an initial turnover of just $500,000 in 1959, Amway is now a multi-national business with a turnover of more than six *billion* dollars in the financial year 1994/1995!

The following list sets out the five skills most frequently used by people rated by their colleagues as outstanding presenters:

> Fine tuning
> Outcome oriented
> Chunking
> Unlimited viewpoints
> Success assurance

- **Fine tuning**
  A skilled presenter constantly hones and refines her material to make it as appropriate as possible for a given audience. This process continues through to the end of the event, and the presenter will use her skill and *flexibility* to adapt the style, tempo and focus of the presentation in order to achieve her original objectives.
- **Achieving outcomes**
  If you don't know where you want to go, how will you know when you've arrived? Top presenters work to answer two basic questions right from the earliest planning stage:
  - What do I want to achieve?
  - How will the audience respond when I am achieving my outcome?
- **Effective chunking**
  'Chunking' is an essential skill which might be described as

the process of 'presenting information in manageable segments'. Some people like to start with an overview and work down to the details while others prefer to start with the details and work up to the big picture.

Skilled presenters most frequently start at a fairly abstract level and chunk downwards. They also watch for audience reactions which will tell them if they are working in the right direction and at the right pace.

● **Unlimited viewpoint**

Many highly rated speakers give their presentations from three different positions. Position 1 is their own viewpoint; Position 2 is the audience's viewpoint; Position 3 is the 'neutral observer' or 'fly on the wall' viewpoint.

By mentally switching from one position to another they can give their presentations a personal dimension (Position 1), they can judge how they are coming across to the audience (Position 2), and can avoid conflict and confrontation, should it arise, by moving to Position 3.

This particular skill takes time to develop, but it is a remarkably effective key to handling any kind of audience and any kind of situation.

● **What *must* be, *will* be**

The fifth characteristic common to most skilful presenters is an unshakeable belief that each presentation is bound to be successful, no matter what happens. It is as though they are constantly repeating to themselves: 'This is the outcome I *require* — therefore it *will* occur.'

It must be seen to be believed

Before you read on, recall an incident from your past which is associated with very strong *positive* emotions — winning a coveted prize, the first time you fell in love, or whatever. Remember as much as you can about the event. Bring to mind the sights, sounds, physical feelings and so on. Then come back to the present and take stock of your state of mind.

How do you feel now? Probably rather more positive than when you started to read this section. Yet nothing actually happened. Your emotional reactions were triggered by a memory, not by an actual event.

You have just demonstrated a very simple form of the technique known as *visualisation*, and its power to generate positive emotions. Visualisation can also be used to focus your efforts more effectively by creating a mental image of a desired event *as though it had already happened*! There is nothing magical about the process, it merely utilises a simple psychological fact:

> The 'middle' or emotional brain cannot tell the difference between an actual experience and a fictional event, be it read, heard, seen or imagined.

Effective visualisation is simply a way of convincing our middle brain that something imagined is, in fact, real. The more vividly we imagine the event, the more the middle brain is convinced that the event must be true – and stores it as a *remembered fact*!

The pudding of proof

Please understand that visualisation is unlikely to work if you try to convince yourself about something you really cannot believe is possible. For the best results, set yourself realistic goals and build upon them as your belief grows.

Concentrate on your own actions and feelings rather than those of your future audience. As a daily activity, build an increasingly detailed mental picture of yourself delivering the presentation in a confident and effective manner.

Tell yourself that you are going to do the best job you can on this presentation, that you are going to be successful, and that you *deserve* that success. You will be amazed at the strength of belief in yourself which develops when you regularly practise the technique.

By the way, you will find that your visualisation is even more effective if you can spend some time in the room where the presentation will take place. If it is at all possible, do take the opportunity to get the 'feel' of the room — its size, the level of any background noise, the seating layout and so on. Stroll around the room as though you owned the place. Do whatever it takes to make your visualisation as realistic as it can be.

Focus your attention on generating positive images and feelings about your role in the presentation. If the whole visualisation process seems a little strange at first, go with it, this is perfectly normal and won't prevent you from achieving a beneficial result. After only a few days you will begin to notice changes in your attitude towards the presentation, and before long you'll actually be looking forward to it.

CHAPTER 4
Confidence Matters

You're never alone in a presentation – it just feels like that

Are you a good letter writer? Do you feel comfortable dealing with people over the phone?

If you answered 'yes' to either of these questions you have already learnt to deal with the presenter's Number One nightmare: *lack of feedback*.

In a face-to-face conversation we are provided with a stream of almost instantaneous signals, both verbal and non-verbal, which let us know how the other person or people in the conversation feel about what we are saying.

During a telephone conversation the physical, non-verbal signals are entirely absent, and we must take our cues from the other person's tone of voice and choice of words. Given that many people have a quite distinct 'telephone manner', even these verbal signals aren't always entirely reliable, however, and this is one of the main reasons why some people prefer not to deal with important and sensitive matters over the phone.

When it comes to writing a letter we get no feedback whatever, of course, which is why so many adults tend to write letters that are nearly as clipped and brief as a telegram.

Delivering a presentation – in terms of the feedback received – ranks somewhere between making a phone call and writing a letter. And that's important, because surveys have shown that most people tend to treat no feedback as *negative feedback!*
Yet there is absolutely no reason why this should be the case.

Martin is giving a presentation at his company's head office. He starts badly, fussing with his OHP foils and vainly trying to get the projected image 'squared up' on the screen. He is clearly ill at ease, and his opening remarks are liberally peppered with 'ums' and 'ahs'.

Then, after the first few minutes, the presentation suddenly begins to improve quite noticeably in pace and clarity. Martin has somehow overcome his initial nervousness and is now in full control of the event.

The only feature of the latter portion of Martin's presentation that seems a little strange is the fact that he looks so long and so frequently towards one particular section of the audience.

Across a crowded room
So what miracle saved Martin's presentation from disaster?
No miracle. Martin simply found a friendly face, someone who was leaning forward in their seat, who appeared to be concentrating on every word he said, and who laughed at all of his humorous asides.

The poor start was primarily due to Martin's feelings of isolation, of being 'on the spot'. He allowed his negative feelings to take the upper hand and showed his lack of confidence. The audience picked up on these non-verbal messages and their body language reflected their own negative feelings. Martin was extremely lucky to find at least one friendly face so that, by establishing a positive rapport with that one member of the audience, he was able to pull himself back from the brink of disaster and deliver a satisfactory presentation.

It's true, then: we aren't really cut off from any kind of feedback when we give a presentation after all — it just feels like that. The real problem is that we get relatively little feedback, and what we do get is of a type that we seldom if ever consciously recognise, namely 'non-verbal signals'.

That certain look

Imagine that you are giving a presentation right this minute. You look out at your audience and you notice that a woman in her mid to late thirties is sitting slightly to your right and has her left leg crossed comfortably over the right so that the left knee is pointing more or less in your direction. Her head is tilted slightly to her right and upwards. Her right hand is resting against her cheek, with the fingers loosely closed, except the index finger, which is pointing straight upwards.

Now, if I say that the woman is looking bright and interested, it won't take much thought to realise that the woman's attitude is positive. But we can actually interpret the meaning of this set (or *cluster*) of body signals much more precisely than that.

The woman's overall deportment is signalling interest and approval. The crossed leg position is only negative when the legs are firmly 'locked', and pointing the upper knee towards someone generally indicates interest. The hand-to-face gesture is a sign of positive evaluation, since the head is not being supported and the mouth is not covered. The head slightly tilted to one side is another indication of interest, as compared to the downward tilted head, which is associated with a negative or critical attitude. The cluster as a whole (and body language must be taken 'as a whole' to have any chance of arriving at an accurate interpretation) says that this member of the audience is on your side, you 'share the same language'.

When you look out at your audience, far from giving you no feedback, they are actually sending you a whole host of messages if only you can recognise them.

Nor do you need to become an expert in reading body language in order to use it as a confidence booster. The only gestures that are worth spotting, in this context, are the positive ones. Like Martin, you should look out for the friendly, approving, interested members of your audience, then work to increase the rapport between those people and yourself. As the enthusiasm builds, because of the *Aura Effect* (see Chapter 14) other members of the audience will find it hard not to become involved.

Of course, body language is not an infallible guide to understanding human behaviour. If someone seems to be half asleep during a presentation it could be just because of a late night. A person who spends the time apparently doodling and who never looks up during the entire presentation may actually be taking notes in some form of shorthand or speed writing.

Make it a habit always to look for the most positive interpretation of any audience behaviour, however odd, or even bizarre, it may be at times. This won't always be easy of course, but you really need to aim to be able to generate confidence from within, rather than depending upon the audience to help you out. And for that you need to *be* confident.

Ready, willing and able

In practice, you would be well advised to start working on any presentation as soon as you have a clear idea of what is required.

Even if you are re-running a previously delivered presentation, check through your materials.

Are your visual aids as clear and interesting as they could be? Have any of the 'facts' in the presentation changed since you last delivered it? Is there anything you can add, remove or alter to make the presentation more interesting, more useful or more appropriate to the next audience?

To have prepared your presentation as fully as possible, with a tightly edited script, sufficient visual aids and plenty of rehearsal time, is a tremendous confidence builder. It will give you a sense of being in control of your material that you can never get from trying to do everything at the last moment.

A sense of perspective

A second key confidence builder is having a realistic appreciation of your *current* strengths and weaknesses.

Decide what kind of presentation you are capable of delivering. Are you happy about using a flipchart, or do you prefer previously prepared foils on an overhead projector? Do you need to work from some kind of cue cards or script, or are you comfortable speaking without notes? If possible, have a chat with someone else in the company whom you regard as being a capable or even talented presenter, and don't be too polite to pick his or her brains.

And finally, when you think you know your own capabilities, try to aim just a bit higher. According to a detailed study carried out some years ago, the average person is successful in approximately 95 per cent of the tasks he or she undertakes. The biggest single cause of failure is not having tried in the first place!

The look, the feel, the sound

We all process our views of the world through a series of filters – audio, visual and sensory. For example, when we are having something explained to us we might say, 'That *sounds* okay to me' or, 'Now I *see* what you're getting at' or, 'That *strikes* me as a good idea'. We unconsciously select our words to express the way we're thinking – our *Preferred Thinking Style* (PTS) – and we respond most positively to people who seem to be using the same filter(s) that we prefer to use – a case of 'seeing eye to eye', 'being in tune' or 'having certain feelings in common'.

A presenter who only uses the phraseology of his own preferred thinking style may be creating a rapport with as few as one-third of the members of his audience. The other two-thirds, though they may never know why, are likely to feel 'out of tune' with the presenter, won't share his 'point of view', or may simply not be able to 'grasp' the meaning of what is being said.

Hand signals should be observed

People frequently make small but easily discernible move-ments that effectively 'point out' their preferred thinking style at a particular moment in time. For example:

- Rubbing or pointing to the area around the eyes indicates a *visual* PTS. That person probably 'doesn't *see* what you're getting at'. Or perhaps she has '*spotted*' something in one of your OHP foils that '*looks* rather interesting'.
- Any noticeable movement around the ears or the mouth indicates an *audio* PTS at work. If someone starts pulling at their earlobe, for example, this may indicate that they don't 'like what they *hear*', but on the other hand, they may be thinking that 'there's a lot in what you *say*'.
- Gestures with the arms and/or hands usually accompany a *sensory* response. That person may '*feel* that the point you have just made needs fleshing out', or they may think that your ideas have given them 'something to get to *grips* with'.

As to whether a particular gesture should be interpreted as a sign of approval or dissent, the expression on the person's face should make that clear for you.

CHAPTER 5
The Main Objective

Is this really necessary?

Not long ago I attended a two-hour presentation for about 60 people, staged by a team of four presenters. The whole event must have taken about 170 hours to prepare and deliver – that's *4.8 working weeks!*

And was it worth it? No. It was poorly structured and over-detailed. The core information could have been presented far more effectively as a four- or five-page memo.

So, always start your preparations by asking yourself: 'Is a presentation the best way of achieving the required objective?' Check it against the following indicators:

- Do people need to be able to discuss the topic of the presentation in order to reach a decision?
- Do people need to be able to question the presenter in order to fully understand the material?
- Is the presentation designed to 'sell' an idea, a product or a course of action?
- Is there any kind of practical element in the presentation?

If there is no obvious need to deliver information in person then staging a presentation may indeed be a second best solution.

Roy was asked to prepare a presentation for some of the senior managers. Unfortunately, he was already under pressure to wrap up an existing assignment, and the time needed to prepare and deliver the presentation could seriously jeopardise the chances of meeting the deadline for the current project. Roy decided to review the situation and examine the *real* goals that he was being asked to achieve, namely to disseminate information.

Instead of preparing a speech, Roy drew up a wholly adequate written description of the required information including half a dozen relevant charts and diagrams. The whole package was put together in a couple of evenings, typed up during the day — while Roy was getting on with his other work — and was delivered to head office a couple of days ahead of the date of the now defunct presentation.

He didn't waste time turning hard facts into a speech, or rehearsing, or preparing visual aids. Nor did he have to be out of the office for a whole day when time was at a premium. The senior managers also benefited in that they were able to review the material at their leisure and didn't have to put off any last-minute appointments that would have clashed with the presentation.

Never assume that a presentation is the only way or the best way to communicate information until you've considered all the other options.

And the point is?

If you do decide that a presentation is necessary, there are at least five or six alternative formats, depending on what you want to achieve. To decide which is most appropriate it helps to start by drawing up a description of your primary objective *in just one sentence*. Something like:

The main point of this presentation is to:

- Inform all the members of the project as to the current state of play.

- Convince senior management that the flexitime system should be extended to include all office staff.
- Explain why the current production targets are unattainable, and to present a more realistic set of figures.
- Motivate the sales force to get behind our latest range of products.

Give this definition of your primary objective some hard thought, and don't go on until you are satisfied that it is as precise and accurate as you can make it. Then stick to it.

Once you know what you aim to say, you are ready to determine what the presentation is meant to achieve. For example:

- To gather people's views — on a new product, on moves to reshape the company, or whatever.
- To make people aware of an idea or to describe a business opportunity — to gain support for some course of action, or to indicate that action will be required in the future.
- To sell something or to persuade people to take a course of action which they might not wish to take.
- To highlight a problem — to seek a solution or at least to minimise its effect.
- To pass on information — to report progress or promote awareness (without requiring any kind of response).
- Education or training — to enhance productivity, encourage a more productive/flexible/efficient work ethic.

Now we need to set out the expected/required *result* of the presentation as clearly as possible.

Hold that thought

No matter why we want to gather people's opinions on any topic, there are certain basic targets that must be set:

- Everyone involved must clearly understand the nature of the presentation.
- Everyone must understand what input is expected from them.

- It is usually more productive in this kind of presentation to have a medium to high degree of audience interaction — to have people build on each other's ideas.
- The presenter(s) must have some kind of yardstick so that they can tell when the presentation has achieved its goals (or at least has gone as far as it can usefully go).

The basic framework for such a presentation might look something like this:

- Introduce the presentation — motivate the audience.
- Describe what is to be discussed, why, and the required objective(s).
- Open the topic up to discussion.
- Summarise the outcome of the discussion.
- If appropriate, give some indication of the likely outcome of the presentation.

I have a dream

When presenting a new idea, your main objectives will be:

- To have the members of the audience clearly understand the new idea.
- To gain acceptance for the new idea.
- To obtain a commitment to implement the new idea.

To achieve these goals the basic outline of your presentation might look something like this:

- Introduce the presentation giving some idea of its purpose — including the need for decision and commitment.
- Describe the *need* for the new idea — does it represent sequential progress or diversification?
- Describe the idea.
- Describe the results and benefits which might reasonably follow the adoption of the new idea.
- Summarise the main points of your presentation and give clear guidelines on what people should do to support the new idea.

Roll up, roll up!

In a sense all presentations are a form of selling — selling information, ideas, solutions and so on. In a deliberately *persuasive* presentation you will need to include some or all of the following elements:

- The members of the audience must understand what is being asked of them.
- They must accept the need for the proposed action.
- Regardless of whether the audience accepts every word of the arguments you are putting forward, they must be persuaded to *act* in the required manner.

This is potentially the most difficult kind of presentation and must be handled with care. Nevertheless, a carefully (and correctly) structured presentation can anticipate any negative reactions and actively encourage your audience to 'buy in' to the proposed action rather than fighting against it:

- Introduction. Briefly identify the subject of the presentation, with strong emphasis on any common interests that may be involved — to keep the business running, to reduce costs, and so on.
- Explain why any action needs to be taken. Be as frank and as open as possible. And if certain information needs to be withheld to protect the company's commercial interests then say so.
- Explain exactly what action needs to be taken, and by whom, showing (if possible) how you have reduced any negative element(s) to a minimum.
- Emphasise the *positive* elements of the course of action.
- Summarise the contents of your presentation and call for agreement on the proposals.

No problem too great

When the key element of a presentation relates to a problem, we might approach it in one of three ways, depending on what we have to say about the problem, and what action (if any) we want from other people:

- Highlight the problem as a matter of information.
- Open the topic up for discussion and possible solutions; or
- Offer a solution to the problem, for further discussion.

In each case our primary aim must be to foster understanding of the problem, and in the last two examples we would also want to:

- Discuss the pros and cons of the possible solutions.
- Gain agreement on what should be done about the problem/solution(s).

The presentation might contain the following elements:

- Introduction. Make it clear whether the presentation is intended simply to highlight the problem, or do you expect some kind of response from the audience?
- Define the problem (including all relevant background and 'historical' information).
- Describe *significant* effects of the problem – who and/or what it affects, how the problem makes itself felt, etc.
- What possible/probable consequences may arise from
  – leaving the problem alone
  – attacking it?

As appropriate:

- Call for suggestions.
- Describe solution(s).
- Recommend preferred solution (and say why it is preferred).
- Call for a decision as to which solution is to be implemented/what further action is to be taken.
- Summarise the main points of the presentation and the discussion, and (where a decision has been reached) indicate what further action will be taken.

Now hear this

The final type of presentation is one designed simply to pass on information – to report progress in a certain area of the company's activities, or just promote general awareness.

Just as all presentations require a degree of salesmanship, they also aim to communicate some kind of information. In this particular type of presentation, however, this is the *primary* aim, with no secondary purpose. The presentation will normally contain the following elements:

- Introduction. Explain what the presentation is about, and what the members of the audience are expected to get out of it.
- Background information which will give the new material a context which makes sense to the audience. This will make the presentation more enjoyable and the new information more memorable.
- A clear and simple description of the new information to provide the framework which will make it as easy as possible for the audience to accept and absorb the data.
- A second review of the information, but this time with supporting evidence/details such as:
  - facts
  - examples (as close as possible to the audience's area of experience)
  - comparisons
  - statistics (but keep them simple)
  - expert opinions (where appropriate).
- Summarise the information, showing how it affects the members of the audience. If the company is moving into new markets, will this mean more work? More money? Greater job security? Show the *whole* picture.

Cutting your cloth

These five presentation outlines are designed to:

- gather opinions;
- publicise an idea or situation;

- sell an idea or course of action;
- highlight a problem (and seek a solution);
- pass on information.

They should be treated as simple templates which can be adapted to fit particular needs and situations. Feel free to pull them about and change them round. Always aim to create presentations in a way that will meet the needs of your audience and which you feel comfortable with. When you feel that a presentation is really yours, that's when your audience will perceive that you are in control of your material. This, in turn, will make them more inclined to accept whatever ideas, plans or information you set before them.

As a practical exercise you might want to scan through the chapter again with the following thought in mind:

Vivian has been asked to do a presentation on a new business opportunity, including a training element so that members of staff can start to work on it within the next few days.
- What elements should she include in her presentation?
- Should the material be split into two separate presentations?
- What would you do?
- What factors would influence your decision?

CHAPTER 6
Know Your Audience

Putting the customer first

If there was ever a time for 'putting the customer first' it *must* be when you are preparing a presentation.

> Ken, from R&D, has to brief the sales team on any new products which his company plans to bring on to the market. Ken hates doing presentations and keeps them as short as possible. He makes few notes and gets one of the secretaries to make up some foils.
>
> The foils are so detailed they are unreadable from more than three feet away. Nevertheless, Ken shows each foil for about 20 seconds (with a brief, jargon-laden explanation of each), there are no handouts, and Ken refuses to take questions.

Strictly speaking, Ken did include all of the information that the sales team needed to know about the new products. But as an exercise in communication the event was a total flop. And Ken hadn't given a second's thought to the people he was supposed to be communicating *with*. The salespeople would have been better off with an audio tape and copies of the foils.

To stage a good presentation it is vital that you concentrate on the basic characteristics of your audience:

- Who will be attending the presentation, and what is their level of seniority/importance?
- Who is the decision maker (where relevant)?
- Is there any point in giving the presentation if certain people are unable to attend?
- Will people be attending your presentation by choice?
- Is their initial attitude likely to be pro, neutral, or anti?
- How intelligent are they? *Never* talk down to people.
- How well informed are they? Will they have any background knowledge at all and, if so, how much?
- Will they understand any jargon you normally use?
- What sort of mood will they be in?
- What will they be expecting from you?
- How can you present your material so as to encourage a positive response (and avoid a negative reaction)?

Every time you can accurately gauge one of these factors, and tailor your presentation accordingly, so your communication will be that much more effective.

Will they hear what you mean?

Do people automatically understand every word you say to them? No such luck!

In real life there is always a 'communication gap' — the difference between what I *meant* to say, what I *actually* said, and what you *think* I said.

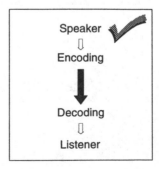

The communication gap

This gap is particularly important when you are delivering a presentation. After all, the word 'audience' is a *collective* noun. It appears to be singular, but it is actually shorthand for 'an audience of individual listeners'.

And not just individuals, but individuals who have a wide variety of views on just about any topic you care to mention.

Let me take a moment to illustrate that point:

Yesterday I watched a child playing with a dog.

What could be more straightforward than this simple sentence? The moment you read those words you understood exactly what they meant – didn't you? Are you sure about that?

See how well you can decode the sentence by answering these questions:

- Was the child a little girl or a little boy?
- What age was the child?
- Where did this event take place?
- What time of day did the event occur?
- What type of dog was the child playing with?
- What colour was the dog?
- Was the dog happy to play with the child?
- Why was I watching the child and the dog – was it my child, or my dog, or both, or neither?

Although we can usually communicate quite easily without cross-checking every word, phrase and sentence, this example shows how much we take language for granted.

See how easy it is to achieve complete misunderstanding with a single word!

The two key ideas we've looked at here are:

- Words are simply a way of expressing the ideas stored in our heads. 'The map is *not* the place', and 'a word is *not* the thing it describes'.
- An audience is a collection of individuals, and must be treated as such.

Audiences have feelings, too

It is always useful, as you prepare a presentation, to consider how it will come across to your audience by asking yourself how they might answer the following questions:

Did you feel that you were being *coerced* or *persuaded*?
Did you feel that you were being *guided* or *manipulated*?
Did you feel *motivated, passive*, or even *uninvolved*?
Did the presenter successfully create rapport with the audience?
Did you feel that there was *any* kind of interaction between you and the presenter?
Did you feel that the presenter gave too much or too little *information*, or just the right amount?
Was there an adequate opportunity to ask questions?
Were your questions fully answered?

Only when you are sure that you have addressed these considerations satisfactorily can you begin to feel that you have produced an effective presentation.

The four learning styles

Every presentation involves some degree of learning, and while you cannot test for the learning mode of every person in the audience you can at least be aware of, and work to, the four basic learning styles:

- The Tortoise – who likes a strong theoretical basis.

- The Philosopher – who learns from practical evidence.
- The Hare – who prefers to learn from hands-on experience.
- The Entrepreneur – who isn't interested in anything but the bare facts.

There are four basic learning styles, which can best be understood in terms of the overall personality, described here in terms of personal style, typical attitude (the motto), how to establish rapport and what they look for in a presentation:

The Tortoise	The Philosopher
Personal Style: Slow but interesting speech Slow moving but not slow witted Avoids eye contact, seldom speaks out voluntarily Tries to fit all new information into existing knowledge base	**Personal Style** Slow speech with very little variation in tone of voice or facial expression Avoids making eye contact Rigid posture Unlikely to speak out, even to ask for clarification
Motto: Today is simply an extension of yesterday	**Motto:** The world would be a better place if it weren't for all the people
To Create Rapport: Speak fairly slowly Don't try to make eye contact Smile a lot (but be sure it's genuine)	**To Create Rapport:** Speak fairly slowly Avoid making eye contact, gesturing or animated speech Show respect for high standards
Presentation Style: Clear, logical structure 'Chunk up' – build up from first principles Support statements with examples and anecdotal evidence	**Presentation Style:** 'Chunk up' – using well-researched, accurate facts Use plenty of examples and anecdotal evidence Give demonstrations wherever possible (and appropriate)

The Hare	The Entrepreneur
Personal Style: Speech is fast and forceful carefully controlled (may be monotonous) May appear loud and abrupt, even aggressive Maintains prolonged eye contact Formal, self-contained posture	**Personal Style:** Can become obsessed with 'The BIG picture' Direct, even forceful, but *not* aggressive Enthusiastic and warm approach to life and people
Motto: Anyone still working at 40 is a failure	**Motto:** If it works, it's good, if it doesn't – move on
To Create Rapport: Speak fairly rapidly, using direct, uncomplicated language Maintain steady eye contact At all costs avoid 'chit chat'	**To Create Rapport:** Speak quickly, using colourful language and anecdotes Vary your tone of voice and adopt an upbeat attitude Be energetic and enthusiastic Always address an entrepreneur by name
Presentation Style: Be brief and succinct 'Chunk down' – give the overall view and a few well-chosen facts Support statements with facts, data and statistics	**Presentation Style:** 'Chunk down' – avoiding all unnecessary details Try to find something unusual about the topic Present in an interesting and lively manner Illustrate your points with examples and stories

Adapt your presentation to these learning styles:

- When *preparing a presentation*, by including material which will appeal to all four learning styles.
- When *taking questions*, by responding to each questioner individually without excluding the rest of the audience.

CHAPTER 7
Words, Words, Words

More than a licence to talk

According to various studies, we can effectively recall:

- 20 per cent of what we hear;
- 30 per cent of what we see;
- 50 per cent of what we hear *and* see;
- 70 per cent of what we do.

The message is clear — to be truly effective an event must allow the audience to see, and hear and interact with the presenter and the presentation material. In practical terms, a presentation must:

- *tell them* what they *need* to know;
- *show them* as much as is necessary to clarify, support and enhance your verbal message;
- create opportunities for *interaction* — and that means more than just allowing time for questions.

Some people find that they can work on all three elements of a presentation at the same time, while others find it easier to write the text, design the visual component, then plan the points of interaction. Experiment and find out which method works best for you. It really doesn't matter which approach you take just as long as you end up with a fully rounded product.

The sweet KISS of success

For every thousand presentations that go on too long, only one or two will be too short. Very few presentations are literally *too short* (in terms of minutes and seconds), which gives a clue to the next secret of producing good presentations:

KISS

In its polite form this stands for *Keep It Short and Simple.*

- In 20 minutes (including the introduction and the conclusion) you have time for only *two* major points.
- In 30 minutes you might make *three* major points.
- In 40–45 minutes you might be able to cover *four* major points, but three points and a longer time for questions would be a better alternative.

Mike Weatherley, one of the producers of the BBC TV programme *Business Matters*, is on record as saying: 'When I'm making a programme, I usually work on the basis that I can get three main points over in the programme.' The fact that a professional TV crew can't get more than three points across in half an hour is surely a lesson for anyone planning a presentation, no matter how sophisticated their set-up.

Something to think about

Most adults have an attention span of somewhere between 25 and 40 minutes, and can only process five to nine chunks of information at any given time. A presentation which contains too many items of information can be too long, even though it lasts for only 15 to 20 minutes. If you speak for much more than 45 minutes, it really doesn't matter how many points you make – most members of the audience will forget almost everything you say within the first couple of hours after you finish speaking!

You need to have the right amount of content, in a reasonable time span, delivered at an acceptable pace.

It's all in the timing

People come to a presentation to gain information which will be useful to them in some way. They come to *learn*, and they need time to *absorb* the new information. Without that time the information won't get past what is called *short-term memory*, and will soon be lost.

The lower line (A) in the diagram below shows the loss of concentration during the middle part of a typical, one-hour presentation. Only the opening (*primary*) and closing (most *recent*) sections are retained to any great extent, and the recovery of attention towards the end of a presentation becomes smaller and smaller, the longer the event goes on.

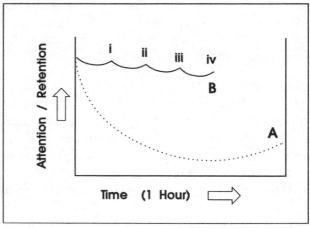

The upper, wavy line (B) shows the effectiveness of a similar presentation – properly structured – with a *maximum* running time of no more than 40 minutes. It really consists of several 'mini-presentations', each with its own lead in and climax. The 'peaks' (i, ii, iii and iv) are built-in *high spots* at 10, 20, 30 and 40 minutes, which actively refocus audience attention, making it easier to maintain concentration between the peak points.

On confronting a blank sheet of paper

A blank sheet of paper that must be filled is one of the most daunting objects on earth, so:

Don't start with a blank sheet of paper.

Yes, I'm serious. I've used this process for years, it is highly efficient and can be learned in a matter of minutes!

The one-man think tank
All you need for this technique is a sheet of plain paper (A4 is okay; A3 size is better), plus a set of coloured pens or pencils.

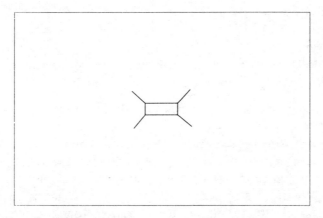

Lay the paper down with one of the long sides towards you and draw a rectangular box in the centre of the page with a line at each corner. (It is even more effective if you draw the central box and the four lines radiating from it in different colours.)

People who plan their presentations by drawing up a list of the things they plan to say often end up with nothing but a censored series of ideas – in no particular order. And if we try to impose some order upon the list – by drawing in linking lines, for example – the end result is even more confused.

The list arrangement (below left) is obviously very poor when it comes to showing relationships *between* points. The spidergram (below right), on the other hand, clearly illustrates individual points *and* the overall structure. What can only be *inferred* from the linked list is made patently obvious in the spidergram:

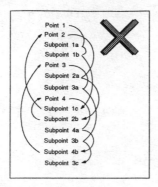 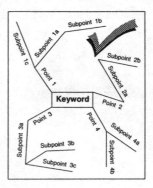

Incidentally, as far as setting out your spidergram is concerned, the following guidelines are recommended:

- The 'keyword' in the central box should be an abbreviation of your primary objective.
- Use just one or two words on each 'limb', even a whole phrase if necessary – but *never* a complete sentence.
- Use the full range of colours you have available.
- If different parts of the spidergram seem to link up, indicate this fact with a linking arrow rather than duplicating a whole set of 'limbs'.

Once you have completed your spidergram you may need to do some serious pruning to bring it back to three main points. It will help to go back to your statement of objectives and start cutting out those parts of your diagram which aren't directly relevant to your primary objective.

All the truth that's fit to present

People tend to respond more readily to upbeat presentations, so concentrate on the *positive* elements of what you want to say and the *negative* aspects of any contrary information. There is nothing wrong in presenting your case in the best possible light so long as you don't use deliberate distortions or lies.

Having said that, you must also allow for people's natural cynicism. If you paint too rosy a picture and avoid all contrary evidence, your audience is likely to become more than a little suspicious. You can actually strengthen your case by including one or two possible objections — which you then demolish — rather than trying to pretend that no objections exist.

Think ahead – plan ahead

Once you think that your basic script is complete, run through it with these three considerations in mind:

- Have you said everything you wanted/needed to say?
- Have you said too much?
- Have you left any obvious hooks for questions?

If necessary, you can now edit your script to resolve any obviously outstanding questions or ambiguous statements, and to remove any 'loose ends'.

You can also script answers to questions that *might* be asked but which you don't want to cover in the presentation.

Script, notes or cue cards?

I once asked a particularly impressive speaker how long it had taken to develop such an effortless, flowing style. The gentleman concerned led me on stage and pointed to the top of the lectern, and some 20 cue cards.

'No one can give a good presentation without doing the preparation,' he told me. 'And very few people are skilled enough to work without some kind of notes.

'What you get from experience isn't the ability to skip the ground work — it's the facility to make it *look* like you didn't have to do the ground work!'

So, which *physical* format is most suitable for your text?

Clearly, your presentation style should match your current level of expertise. How good is your memory under pressure, for example? It may look very professional if you appear to be speaking 'off the cuff', but how professional will it look if you say 'Next Monday' when you mean 'A week on Monday', or if you say '27 per cent' when you should have said '72 per cent'?

Some people really can produce a speech at the drop of a hat. Most of us need some form of script.

Full script

A full script takes time to prepare since it must be more or less word perfect. If you don't happen to have a professional scriptwriter on hand, you may have to produce several drafts before you get your script worded entirely to your satisfaction.

Using a full script can be a great confidence builder. You cannot forget your lines; there is no danger of leaving something unsaid or of giving incorrect information; and you can time your presentation with considerable accuracy.

On the minus side, it is exceedingly difficult to *write* a script that sounds natural, let alone *read* a script so that it sounds natural. You must constantly break eye contact in order to look down at your script, and you are more or less tied to the lectern or whatever your notes are resting on.

Tip:
Modularise your script. Write it so that you can add or remove material in neat chunks if the need arises.

A word-for-word text is also notoriously inflexible. If any part of your script needs to be changed at the last moment you'll just have to cross out the obsolete material and make do with what is left — or learn to write very fast!

Notes

It is not unknown for a speaker to use a mind map as the 'notes' for a presentation. It is more common, however, to prepare notes with main headings, subheadings and a brief outline of each point that you wish to make. In short, a rough guide to what you want to say.

Using notes means that you have something down in black and white (for confidence building), and in a format that can easily be edited right up to the last moment. If time runs short, you can use the same material, but simply deal with each point in less detail.

Notes also allow you to *appear* more spontaneous, since you really will be speaking 'off the cuff', to a certain extent.

The main drawback to using notes is that it is entirely up to you to remember what you meant to say about a particular heading or subheading. You will also need a place where you can rest your notes so that you can see them, but the audience can't.

Cue cards

Since cue cards (box file cards, approximately 10cm x 15cm, for example) are much smaller than A4 sheets of paper, you will need to work with key *words* and *phrases* rather than sentences.

> **Tip:**
> To avoid getting your cue cards mixed up, number them distinctly in one corner. Or punch a hole in one corner of each card so that they can be held together by a treasury tag or similar fastening.

Using cue cards means that you can carry part of your script with you if you want to move away from the lectern. This will give you virtually unlimited freedom of movement.

The main drawback to using cue cards is the lack of written information. All the cards for a single presentation should fit easily into a jacket pocket or handbag. If they don't, your presentation may be too long, or you're putting too much on your cue cards. Perhaps you would be more comfortable using notes?

Visual aids as memory joggers

Using the visual aids as an abbreviated script cuts down on preparation and allows a great deal of flexibility. But you will need to check each visual as you display it, which *could* mean that you spend more time looking at the displays than at the audience. You should also avoid making the visual aids more detailed to compensate for the lack of script or notes.

Foil backing sheets

If you have foils with backing sheets, these can be used:

- to carry a copy of the contents of the foil;
- for notes regarding the contents of the foil.

As your presentation skills develop, you may find that this is a practical alternative to the options suggested above.

CHAPTER 8
When You Come to the End – Stop

The intro and the outro

The two parts of your presentation that will be remembered most clearly are the introduction and the conclusion – especially the conclusion. A good ending can sometimes turn a rather mediocre presentation into a success. Likewise, a bad ending can ruin an otherwise excellent presentation, leaving the audience feeling dissatisfied and critical rather than impressed and appreciative.

Always aim to finish a presentation (no matter what the subject) on a positive note. Make the audience feel that you and they have shared a worthwhile experience. In the old show business adage, 'Always leave them wanting more.'

The second reason can be summed up in the phrase: every presentation needs a clear, well-planned *outcome*.

What was it all about?

We've already seen how a presentation should be structured in line with its purpose, its outcome. The closing section of a presentation is a vital part of that structure, and must be something more than just the end of the event. It must summarise all that has gone before and create a bridge to whatever happens after the presentation is all over.

What your audience will really need to know is:

What (are we supposed to do)?
When (do we do it)?
How (will we know when we've done it satisfactorily)?

The answers to these questions depend on the intended outcome of the presentation, of course, and your closing remarks should aim to answer the questions as precisely and clearly as possible.

Closing comments

Three common errors that occur when closing a presentation are:

The emergency stop

Without a hint of warning the speaker pulls up, in a metaphorical screech of brakes, with a phrase such as:

Well, I think that's all I have to say, so I'll stop there.

The speaker 'thinks' she has nothing more to say? Didn't she draw up some kind of script? Doesn't she *know* that she has nothing more that needs saying? Maybe she's left something out, but how will the audience ever know?

By the time you come to the end of a presentation you should have answered the three vital questions: What?, When? and How?, and there should be no need to announce the fact. Nor is it necessary to offer a self-evident observation such as: 'I've finished so I'll stop.'

If you have finished, unexpectedly or not, leave it at that and either invite questions or sit down, depending on how the event has been arranged.

The endless maze

The 'endless maze' speaker can be recognised by the way that he ends up as lost and confused as his audience, thus:

And so I'll finish on that point and remind you of the comment I made earlier about ...

And off he goes again.

It's as though he is lost in some kind of oral maze, frequently sighting the exit but never quite able to reach it before veering off down another detour.

This speaker also isn't working from a well-prepared script or he would have no trouble reaching the exit. Presumably, he simply threw a few ideas together at the last moment, and now he's hoping that if he talks for long enough he is bound to cover all the bases, sooner or later.

The clichéd climax

Unlike the 'emergency stop', where the speaker seems to arrive at an ending by accident, the 'clichéd climax' presenter obviously knows exactly when she's going to finish – and insists on broadcasting the fact:

In conclusion ...
Just before I close ...
And finally ...
I'd like to leave you with this thought ...

It's as though the speaker wants to prepare us for that terrible moment when she will stop speaking and all the joy will go out of our lives.

The more the merrier

All of these examples clearly illustrate the need for a well-ordered structure in any presentation. Not just because it seems like a good idea, but because it saves so much trouble in the long run – as in the case of the style of ending I've dubbed 'the more the merrier'.

Favourite phrases this time include:

And in addition ...
I'd also like to say/point out/remind you ...

When a 'more the merrier' speaker reaches the end of a presentation it is not an ending after all, but a new beginning. It seems that the process of summing up his ideas generates a whole series of new thoughts. The audience, on the other hand, can only remain attentive for a limited amount of time.

Last-minute ideas, no matter how brilliant, should be saved for another day unless they genuinely dovetail into the points set out in your script – and are essential to the effectiveness of the presentation.

Know when to stop

Speakers often fall into 'endless maze' or 'more the merrier' mode when they find that they have finished ahead of time and thereby snatch defeat from the very jaws of success.

To put it bluntly, few presentations fail by ending early – unless the premature ending is due to lack of adequate preparation. If you can say everything you want and/or need to say in less than your allotted time, that is a bonus, not an error. Don't spoil the effect by trying to pad your speech up to the 'official' length. Make the most of the situation by allowing an extended question and answer session or by inserting an extra comfort break.

Happy endings

Having described some 'presentation pitfalls', let's move on now to get some ideas on how it *should* be done:

The closing summary

A closing summary, though useful in almost any setting, is most suitable when the presentation itself is only intended to communicate information and doesn't require any follow-up activity by the members of the audience. Carefully avoiding clichés such as:

> So, before I finish, I'd just like to summarise the points we've covered this afternoon ...

you can proceed straight into the summary with no introduction at all, as in:

> So, we've seen what kind of pressures the company faces (*list the*

pressures), and the possible ways in which those pressures can be handled *(list the alternatives)* ...

The challenge
Issuing a challenge to the audience is used to best effect where a particular problem has been addressed, or where you are calling for greater or renewed effort.

Couch the challenge in terms of what 'we can' do, or 'we will' do, and state a precise course of action in this context. A mere emotional appeal for some (unspecified) action may be very rousing at the time, but it is likely to lead to confusion and/or apathy when the members of the audience actually try to put your rhetoric into practice.

The 'call to action'
When the main intention is to generate agreement on a particular course of action you may find it more effective to use persuasion rather than a challenge, and to this end it is valid to confine your summation to the points *in favour* of the proposed action and to end by stating precisely what the next step should be.

Since you will presumably have covered any contradictory arguments – and answered them – in the course of your presentation, it is unnecessary to state them all over again. One of the most oustanding examples of a *call to action* ending was used at the climax of a political rally when the party leader exhorted his followers to: 'Go home and prepare to rule!'

As it turned out, the call was somewhat over optimistic. No matter. It's purpose was to create a positive attitude, and in this respect it was hugely successful.

The 'feel good' factor
Motivational speakers aim to leave the audience with a warm glow rather than indicating some further course of action. This would work well in the closing session of a multi-presentation event where you wish to reinforce the group identity, for example, but is out of place at a relatively impersonal event such as a press conference.

The two most popular forms of the 'feel good' ending make use of a quotation or a piece of poetry respectively. In both cases the material should be short and to the point, though the 'point' in question does not have to be directly linked to the subject of the presentation. As long as the material is highly emotionally charged, the precise nature of the quotation or poem will be dictated by the emotional response you wish to arouse in your audience, rather than by the subject of the presentation.

Beware the red light

If you've ever watched a political conference on TV you've probably noticed the coloured lights that are used to signal to speakers when their time is up. You may also have noticed how often speakers start to panic when the warning light comes on, despite the fact that they must surely have known how much time they would have when they were preparing their speech.

It sometimes happens that jokes get more laughs and bold declarations get more applause than speakers expect, which throws their timing out. A well-prepared speaker always arms himself with *two* copies of his closing comments.

One copy is based on the assumption that nothing unforeseen will happen, and the speaker will have all the time that he needs to wrap up the presentation at his own speed. The second copy (the copy that most speakers overlook) is set out on the basis that everything that can go wrong *will* go wrong and that he will need to wind up his comments in very short order indeed.

The length of the 'emergency' ending will depend on the length of the presentation as a whole. If your entire speech lasts only five or ten minutes then allow one or two minutes for your long ending, and 30–45 seconds for the emergency ending. If your presentation is scheduled for 30–40 minutes (or more!) then the two endings would be longer – but not too much longer.

CHAPTER 9
Curtain Up!

The 'magic minute'

Within 5–10 *seconds* of your entrance every member of your audience will have formed a subconscious opinion of you. In the next 50–55 seconds that opinion will be confirmed, or perhaps qualified, but almost never undone!

The members of an audience react to everything they see and hear, and the overall impact of a presentation will be enhanced by anything up to 18 or 20 per cent by a well-judged introduction. It must first act as a 'hook' to catch your audience's attention, and then go on to:

- command attention;
- create a framework;
- set the mood;
- create motivation;
- establish credibility;
- summarise your message;
- indicate whether batteries are included;
- set out your time lines.

Let's start, then, by looking at some of the different kinds of 'hooks'.

Quotations
There are a number of excellent books of quotations on the market, but be sure to select a quote that is appropriate, and from someone who will have credibility with your audience:

'As Winston Churchill once said ...'
'As Mabel Ramsbotham once observed ...'

Most people have at least a vague idea that Winston Churchill was someone famous and important. But who cares what Mabel Ramsbotham once observed? Unless, of course, she is a well-respected colleague, a department head or the managing director, in which case her opinion may well count for a lot more than the thoughts of Winston Churchill.

Humour

There are two basic forms of humour — *instinctive* and *deliberate*. Instinctive humour grows out of the presentation material — the sort of humour 'you had to be there to appreciate'.

Deliberate humour, on the other hand, encompasses jokes, funny stories, cartoons and so on. If you're seriously considering using 'deliberate' humour in your presentation, I suggest that you think long and hard — and then change your mind. One genuinely funny, *relevant* story will work far better than half a dozen jokes.

The important questions to ask yourself about *any* kind of humour are:

- Will people understand it (as you intended it)?
- Will they find it funny?

If you're not sure on either count, try something else.

Questions

Asking a question right at the start of a presentation is a good way of letting your audience know that you wish to communicate *with* them, rather than simply lecture *at* them.

For the best effect ask the audience a question that only allows for an unqualified 'Yes/No' answer (preferably 'Yes'), such as 'Can you hear me at the back?'

Also make sure that you are asking for a manageable response. The question: 'Is the seating comfortable?' is certainly relevant. But what do you do if a majority of the audience answer 'No'?

Visual impact

You could wait until everyone is seated, then leap on to the stage wearing a gorilla suit and waving a bunch of bananas. Or then again, maybe not. Many people still believe that 'clothes make the man – or woman', and they will happily judge you on your physical appearance – and nothing else. If you want people to take notice of what you have to say, dress as far as possible to meet your audience's expectations.

Topical references

Topical references can be used to great effect, as long as they are genuinely relevant to the subject under discussion.

Personal anecdotes

These must be *very* appropriate, and appropriately brief, to justify their use. I once attended a presentation where the speaker opened with a personal anecdote that started: 'You know, I nearly didn't live long enough to make this presentation ...'

At that moment he had the absolute attention of everyone in the room. Three or four minutes later, as he struggled to the end of his story, most people were thinking, 'So what?'

Shocking statistics

If you want to use a shocking statistic – to get your audience's attention without actually insulting them – then make it as simple but as hard-hitting as possible. Something like:

> 'Seventy-five per cent of all retired people are living on a greatly reduced income. Thirty per cent of all retired people are living on or below the poverty line. The material we're going to cover in this presentation could save you becoming a part of those statistics!'

Used well, shocking statistics can be extremely effective, as long as you remember that statistics are easily misunderstood, unless the information is kept short and simple.

Outrageous statements

Speaker (*to audience of computer programmers*): 'Do you realise that you are wasting your time if you don't have a decent technical author to prepare your documentation?'

[*Short pause*]

'At least, that's how your customers may see it.'

From the audience's point of view this was definitely a highly contentious opening, but it achieved its purpose.

The 'outrageous statement' opening will undoubtedly make your audience sit up and take notice, and if it (gently) ruffles a few feathers, it may also help the audience to remember the message when a more gentlemanly, neutral presentation has long since faded from memory.

Teasers

One trainer I used to work with liked to have the following four instructions written up on a flipchart or whiteboard before the delegates started to arrive:

- Make mistakes
- Ask 'dumb' questions
- Cheat
- Have fun

Once the delegates were assembled he would explain that the four points meant:

- Nobody is perfect, so understand that making mistakes is a valuable element in the learning process.
- If you don't understand something, say so.
- Forget everything you learned in school about not looking at other people's work. In business we work best when we pool our knowledge.
- Treat this course as an *opportunity*, not as an obligation. The more you enjoy the course, the more effectively will you absorb the course material.

Maps and shoehorns

Once your audience is satisfactorily 'hooked' there are other functions an introduction must serve.

In some situations it will be more appropriate to calm and reassure your audience rather than trying to get them stirred up. One way of doing this might be to 'draw a map' of the 'territory' you intend to cover in your presentation. That is, to provide a summary of what is to follow in a reassuring manner.

It is also an effective way of dealing with a situation where you know that different members of the audience have quite different views on the main topic of the presentation. In this case, the purpose of the 'mapping' process is to provide a clear, definitive view of the topic. You can't expect everyone to fall in line with your definition automatically, of course, but at least it will be plain to all concerned just where the presentation is coming from.

Just how detailed your map needs to be will depend on how much (relevant) prior knowledge your audience have. In some situations the people in your audience may have nearly as much information as you have yourself, in which case it is simply a question of fleshing out that knowledge so that they can make a decision, undertake a particular course of action, or whatever.

If you find that your audience knows little or nothing about the subject of the presentation then your initial map must be more detailed than normal. But not so detailed that it becomes a summary of everything that you are going to talk about.

Think of it rather as a shoehorn, helping to ease the audience into the subject. Introduce some small part of your topic by relating it to something that the members of the audience will already know about and which matters to them. This will reassure them that your topic is comprehensible, and that the presentation is relevant to their current situation/ future needs. It will also give them the confidence to follow along even if things get a little complicated and technical later on.

Setting a mood

How do you want your audience to feel as the presentation starts? Relaxed? Alert? Critical? Receptive?

Your opening remarks will play a crucial role in setting the mood of the whole presentation. Would you open a presentation with a shocking statistic or statement if you wanted the audience to feel relaxed and receptive? Would you try to stir your sales force to greater efforts by the use of soft lights and a 'fireside chat'?

For maximum effect you must analyse your audience as far as possible, and then make a best guess as to what kind of approach will produce the required response from that particular set of people. Above all, *never* assume that any two audiences will react the same way to the same material; they won't.

Creating motivation

The best way to motivate your audience can be summed up in the question, 'What's in it for me?'

This may seem rather mercenary, but as Dale Carnegie points out in *How to Win Friends and Influence People*, self-interest is an incredibly effective source of motivation.

To make people take notice of what you have to say, give them a reason to listen, a reason which relates to their own experience.

Talk to your audience as they are, not as you would like them to be. This, too, will benefit from as much audience analysis as you can manage. Some members of your audience may have been 'volunteered', rather than choosing to come of their own accord. Don't let this put you off. It may actually be easier to sell the presentation to those people if you can only show them that they aren't going to be wasting their time after all.

American psychologist Abraham Maslow has described what might be called a *hierarchy of motivation*:

The pyramid represents various levels of achievement. People can only be motivated to move up to the next level when they have satisfactorily met the basic requirements of their current level. You are unlikely to have much success encouraging a company to embark on a major reorganisation when their most pressing need is to find enough money to pay their suppliers!

For maximum effect, then, you must *engage* your audience's attention at their *current* level, and then show them how your presentation will fulfil their natural desire (according to Maslow) to move up to the next level of motivation.

Establishing credibility

Establishing your credentials is a surprisingly delicate affair. A string of academic and/or professional qualifications, and details of your years as the right hand of God may sound impressive, but you are far more likely to achieve rapport if you adopt a style of introduction that is more gentle on your audience's self-respect.

Are batteries included?

Always let your audience know whether some kind of follow-up action will be expected of them, and how they can tell when they have successfully completed the required task. The phrase 'Sales must rise' may sound terrific at the time, yet it really doesn't say very much at all. How much must sales rise by? Over what period of time?

Making and breaking expectations

It is always a good move to show your audience that you are aware of their expectations, and to clear up any misconceptions that you know or believe exist regarding the reason(s) for the presentation. Let your audience know that you are all there for a common purpose and see how it builds rapport.

Providing a framework

People find it easier to absorb new information if they can relate it to the knowledge they already possess – hence the repetitive nature of the guideline:

Tell them what you're going to tell them.
Tell them.
Tell them what you've told them – and why.

Always aim to use your introduction to create a bridge from the audience's existing knowledge to your *new* information.

Times and events

Where several presentations follow on from one another, set people's minds at rest (and thereby make them more receptive) by explaining the total situation, not just your part of it.

Some presenters talk through a foil listing events and times. Alternatively, you might include a timetable as part of the initial handout and then use a foil to confirm that everything will go as planned, or to explain any alterations to the programme.

Incidentally, when you say your presentation will last for

10, or 20 or 30 minutes, make sure it doesn't run for 15, 25 or 35 minutes.

Never say not!

Human beings cannot think in negatives. If I say, 'I'm *not* here to sell you anything', your subconscious mind hears: 'I'm here to sell you anything – not' which means that by the time you get to 'not' you've already heard me say that I *am* here to sell you something!

So, if there's something you don't want the audience to think about, *leave it out*. If you say it, they'll think about it, no matter how carefully you phrase it.

CHAPTER 10
Selecting and Using Visual Aids

Just for effect?

Why use visual aids? Just consider the following facts:

- We learn about 90 per cent of what we know *visually* – from films, books, etc. Only 7 to 11 per cent is learnt through hearing alone.
- The average audience member will remember about 70 per cent of a purely verbal presentation three hours later, and as little as 10 per cent only three days later.
- Of a purely visual presentation, about 75 per cent will be remembered after three hours, and up to 20 per cent after three days.
- About 85 per cent of a mixed verbal/visual presentation will be recalled after three hours, and as much as 66 per cent will be remembered after three days.
- Presenters who use visual aids are generally perceived as being more professional and persuasive than those who rely on speech alone.

In short, for a truly powerful *and memorable* presentation you will need to include some form of visual aid.

Horses for courses

Having stated the advantages, it is only fair to point out that visual aids can only be justified when used well. From the options available to you, think very carefully about which form of visual aid will best suit your purpose, your audience and your own skill. (Different visual aids should never be used simultaneously, unless you have professional assistance.)

Chalkboard

'Chalk and Talk' is rapidly becoming a synonym for the most ineffective, hidebound form of training. While this medium is certainly cheap, it is also extremely limited and really only suitable for small groups (a dozen or less), and where more modern facilities are not available.

Whiteboard and pen

Although a whiteboard shows colours far more effectively than a chalkboard, you will still need to have presentable handwriting to make the best use of this medium. If in doubt, always use block capital letters, not 'joined up' lettering.

Whiteboards are suitable for informal meetings such as discussion groups and brainstorming, and for ad hoc displays in formal meetings (as an alternative to a flipchart). Audience size (around 20–30) will depend on the quality of your writing.

Tip:
Some whiteboard/flipchart pens use a spirit-based ink which evaporates very easily when exposed to the air, so always put the cap back on a pen as soon as you stop writing.

One of the main drawbacks to using a whiteboard is the lack of any permanent record of what was written/drawn on the board once it has been cleaned off, though electronic whiteboards are now available which will give an A4-size printout of the current contents of the writing area.

Flipcharts

Flipcharts can be a mixed blessing. They are relatively cheap, but can be hard to handle. They are suitable for multicoloured displays, but some types of ink tend to 'bleed' through flipchart-type paper. Once again, the presenter's handwriting skills will affect the advisability of using this medium. If you usually have to decipher your writing for other readers, avoid flipcharts.

Flipcharts can be used to great effect with groups of up to 30 people, especially when it is necessary to record lists of ideas or display 'spur of the moment' information.

Individual pages and sequences can be prepared in advance and/or built up as the presentation goes along, and pages can be torn out and stuck up on the wall with Blu-tack to create an expanding display.

Overhead projector (OHP)

The OHP has become one of the most widely used visual aids in business presentations. Given an adequate screen and appropriate seating arrangements, it is suitable for almost any size of audience up to 500 or more.

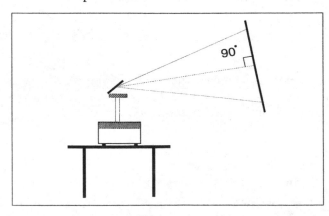

Because of the OHP the screen should, ideally, be at right angles to a line drawn from the centre of the screen to the centre of the projection mirror (see illustration), a wall, even a plain white one, is *not* an entirely satisfactory alternative to a proper screen.

As a general rule, the size of screen for a given venue can be calculated using the ratio of 1:6; thus, if the last row of seats is 42 feet from the screen, the screen should be 42/6 = 7 feet square. (Minimum screen size should be about 5 feet square.)

Foils are a very flexible medium, and are suitable for formal or informal presentations, especially where any type of graphical information is involved.

The main advantages of an OHP are its ease of use and the option of switching between various display styles. Foils may be used:

- In straight display mode where the entire foil is immediately visible.
- As a sequence of overlays, to build up a complex picture.
- In 'progressive revelation' fashion, whereby points are revealed by sliding a mask down the foil.

The main disadvantage of using an OHP is the difficulty of ensuring that everyone can see the whole screen:

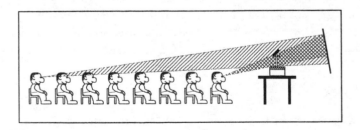

This situation is almost inevitable unless the OHP is correctly positioned on a purpose-built stand. This is the main reason why you should never use the whole area of an OHP foil.

- Text on an OHP foil should be *at least* 6–7 millimetres in height (that's between 24pt and 28pt), and will need to increase to about 15 millimetres (or 60pt) if any part of the audience will be more than 30–40 feet away from the screen (4pts = 1 millimetre (approx.) or $\frac{1}{18}$ inch).

- Always use foils in the 'landscape' position to minimise poor visibility, and leave a margin of about one inch on all four sides of the foil. Do not use the bottom third of the foil at all if you can possibly avoid it.

- Ten to twelve words on each foil is a sensible maximum. If a foil is too 'busy' your audience will happily ignore what you are saying until they have read the foil all the way through (or until you move on to the next foil).

The foil on the left is actually subdivided under four separate headings. The foil on the right shows the first heading set out correctly (the rest of the left-hand foil should be divided into three further foils, following the same basic guidelines).

Slides

Slide projection is a medium suitable for audiences of almost any size up to 1000 or more, but again depends on screen size and the power of the projector.

The slides themselves can be relatively expensive to produce, though well-produced slides, properly used, will bring a tangible air of professionalism to any presentation. Many computer graphics packages have the capacity to produce high quality visuals which can be transferred to slides.

For larger audiences this medium is undoubtedly one of the best ways of presenting all types of information.

Tip:
Every time you turn the projector on and off, you increase the likelihood of bulb failure. Avoid the problem by displaying a neutral slide (the company logo, for example) rather than switching the projector off.

Incidentally, slide displays work best when the room is *almost* totally blacked out. Unfortunately, these conditions are also ideal for falling asleep, especially after lunch.

Computer-based displays

There are, in fact, not one but three ways of utilising computer-generated displays in a presentation context:

1. Connecting a computer to one or more large-screen TVs is simple, practical and extremely cost effective.
2. Purchase or hire a video projection package – a large screen (about 5 feet square) with surround, a three-colour video projector, and the computer, remote control, connecting cables, etc.
3. An LCD projection panel, coupled with an OHP, will allow you to project an enlarged version of an ordinary computer screen.

In a well-equipped setting, including multiple screens, it should be quite possible to cater for audiences of 100 or more delegates.

The ideal situation for using a computer-based display is one where it is necessary that the audience see a computer application up and running. This would typically be where a new piece of software is being demonstrated for sales or training purposes.

Alternatively, using a product such as Microsoft's *Power-*

point, you can create a dynamic presentation which runs itself and which can be tailored to the needs of a specific audience.

Tip:
Always run a pre-presentation check and don't change anything once the display is working satisfactorily. When using an LCD panel, make sure that the projector light is bright enough.

The computer/TV set up and the LCD projection panels can be used in almost any setting, and virtually at a moment's notice, while the video projection equipment is really only suitable for larger, properly stage-managed, pre-planned events.

The biggest drawback to using any kind of *projected* computer output is the cost. Both options will run to several hundred pounds per day to hire, or thousands of pounds to buy outright.

Video

Video tape technology, when used well, can add an invaluable air of professionalism to what would otherwise be no more than an adequate presentation. It can be used for both formal and informal meetings, product presentations, training sessions, etc. Video is not appropriate where the information has a high text and/or numerical content.

Without special equipment a video presentation is limited to an audience of no more than 20–30, but this figure jumps to several hundred using a high powered video projector or multiple screens.

Tip:
Always run a video tape *right through* the night before you intend to use it. Nothing is worse than to find that a tape is in first class condition except for a loss of picture and/or sound right in the middle of an important statement or explanation.

Try making your own video presentation and you will quickly discover why a professionally produced video costs so much to make. Pre-recorded videos, on the other hand, can be hired from a number of companies at reasonable cost. The videoed presentation is particularly appropriate, and cost-effective, when you want to get the same information or message to several different groups at a number of separate events.

Film

Most of the information that once came on film – training materials, health and safety presentations, company PR material, etc, are now available on video instead. And why not? Video tape is both easier to use and much cheaper than film.

Having said that, film has the advantage that it can be used as easily in small groups or for an audience of thousands (depending on use of appropriate equipment and screen size). Despite the relatively high production costs, a well-made film still carries a high 'impressiveness' rating, which makes it particularly suitable for large, formal presentations such as AGMs, product launches, etc.

> **Tip:**
> Film can be quite delicate, especially hire films which have seen extensive use. If it is at all possible, always have an experienced projectionist on hand (even for small, in-house presentations).

The great weakness of film is its inflexibility. Once a film is ready for showing it cannot easily be changed without incurring considerable expense. Creating back-up copies is impossible without the use of expensive professional facilities.

CHAPTER 11
Designing Effective Visual Aids

Planning screen and flipchart displays

A foil or slide is most productive if it is a focus of attention. A display with three or four bullet points, with three to five words per point, will be far more efficient than a screen full of text.

The following exercise is designed to help you to make your foils as simple yet as powerful as possible:

1. Produce a foil which contains *all* the points and details which you think should be on it.
2. Project the foil and time yourself to see how long it takes to read *everything* on the foil.
3. If it takes much more than five seconds to read a particular foil or slide then it needs editing!
4. Check to see how much of the text (if any) is simply a copy of part of your spoken material.
5. Cross out everything that isn't *absolutely necessary*. If you still have anything larger than key words/phrases, you haven't finished editing.
6. If more than four to five bullet points are left, either merge some of the points or split them up over several foils.
7. If a rehearsal leaves you changing foils almost as fast as you can speak, your bullet points are too detailed. Replan your foils so that the bullet points are less specific.

Points that make a point

Why do so many presenters depend on a series of anonymous black bullet points? In a book like this, black bullets are fine, but in a situation where each display stays up for a minute or more it is worth replacing the standard 'black blob' with something more creative:

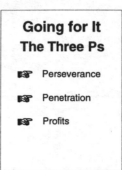

These two foils are actually pure text, and text can be used just like graphics. In the next example it is the *visual* impact which makes the display so effective (the top line reads: 'Verbal Content = 7 per cent'):

verbal content = 7 per cent

Vocal Interest = 38 per cent

Body Language = 55 per cent

We could present the same information in more scientific manner using a pie chart:

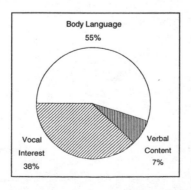

or we can make it more eye-catching by using a touch of humour:

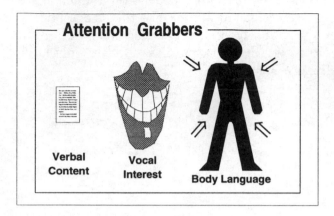

A chart (or graph) for all reasons

Charts and graphs can be an invaluable way of presenting numerical data in an easily understood format. But what is the *best* way of illustrating a particular piece of information?

- **KISS** (Keep It Short and Simple). If the audience does not get the message in five to ten seconds, they'll be watching the screen when they should be listening to you.
- Careful use of colours makes the information more interesting and more memorable.
- Use four lines per graph at most, and use a different colour for each line if the graph shows more than one line.

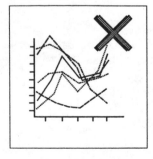

- *Line graphs* are best suited to illustrate trends over a period of time such as 'rolling' sales figures and so on. They are not suitable for illustrating precise values.
- Avoid *vertical* labels in a line graph. They are hard to read and therefore easily misread.

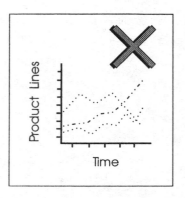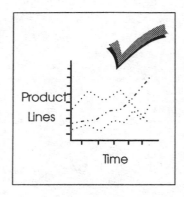

- To minimise the differences in a line graph, make the Y *axis* (the base line) as long as possible (within reason).
- To maximise the differences in a line graph, make the X (vertical) *axis* as long as possible.

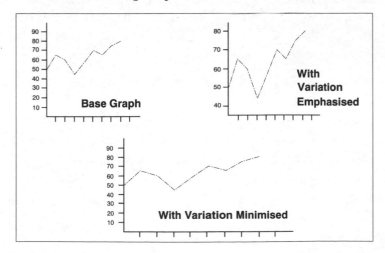

- In any kind of *bar chart*, limit each display to six or seven bars (or groups of bars) at the most.
- Use a *vertical bar chart* (with bars running from top to bottom) to compare related data at several points in time.
- It is sometimes quite difficult to see exactly what is going on in a *'stacked' bar chart*.
- Use 'stacked' columns if the precise make-up of each column is relatively unimportant, otherwise groups of adjacent bars are more effective.

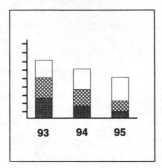 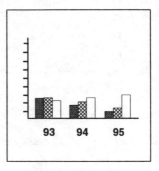

- A *horizontal bar chart* (histogram) is best suited to showing relative values for a number of related items at a given moment in time and where the main purpose of the chart is to illustrate relative values.

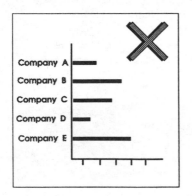 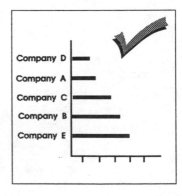

- When using a histogram, *always* arrange the bars in ascending or descending order of magnitude, not in alphabetical order.

- A *pie chart* is often the best way of illustrating the relative values which go together to make up a single whole (how a given market is currently shared out between the various manufacturers, for example).

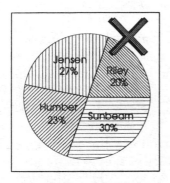 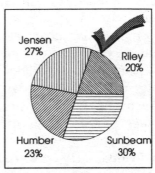

- Always put the labels for a pie chart *outside* the chart.
- Keep pie charts down to six or seven wedges. If necessary, group some of the less important or very closely connected items under a single heading.
- Use a 'floating wedge' when you want to focus attention on that particular section of the pie (and never use more than one floating wedge per chart).

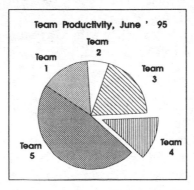

Handouts

A handout, be it text, graphics or both, provides a *visual* reinforcement for the other elements of a presentation.

Quite apart from the difficulties of ensuring that your audience accurately interpret your message, a quarter of the population have an *auditory* PTS (Primary Thinking Style) and they will appreciate the opportunity to read through the handout as you are speaking in order to understand the points that you are making!

The other 75 per cent need that back-up material or there are likely to be significant gaps in their version of what you said – which will be filled in with what they think you probably said.

Those members of the audience who have a high level of *right brain* activity may find it relatively difficult to stay attentive if your presentation follows the usual progression from individual facts up to overall picture. An interesting and imaginative handout will help to focus their attention.

In short, a handout ensures that your audience get the message, the whole message and nothing but the message.

But when should you hand out the handouts: before, during or after the presentation?

- *Before* – you really have no control over what people do with the handout.
- At the start of each *subsection* of an event – some people may read ahead, but at least they will be limited to material that is to be covered within the current session.
- *After* – no one can read ahead.

On the other hand:

- People don't usually read the handout unless they are bored with the presentation.
- If the presentation is mainly a detailed explanation of the foils in the handout, people will appreciate being able to make notes directly alongside the relevant illustrations.
- It is a presenter's job to produce an interesting and informative presentation – not to police the audience.

The key factor which decides when to circulate a handout is purely utilitarian: when should it be distributed to achieve the greatest benefit for the maximum number of people?

And then the lights went out

What would you do if your entire presentation revolves around some kind of electrical equipment and at the very last moment it all breaks down?

Worse still, what are you going to do if something goes wrong with the equipment during your presentation?

● You can panic.
● You can fall back on *Plan B*.

Any presenter who works with electrical devices should always have a Plan B. With a good Plan B, you can carry on regardless (using a different medium), instead of grinding to a humiliating halt as you hear that delicate 'pop' of exploding equipment.

Your personal Plan B will depend on which visual aids you are using, but here is one of the most common back-up systems.

No matter whether you're using an OHP or slide projector, a video or a film, be sure to duplicate all your main displays on a flipchart (flipcharts never blow a fuse or a bulb).

This means extra work, of course, but if you ever have to fall back on Plan B it will save your presentation and your face.

And if nothing goes wrong? Then at least you will have had the reassurance that you were prepared for any eventuality.

CHAPTER 12
Setting the Scene

Anyone for tennis?

When it comes to setting up your display facilities – flipchart, OHP or slide projector, etc – there are two basic options. The first alternative – the 'head on' position – places the screen directly facing the audience. The second option requires that the screen be placed to one side and at an angle to the audience.

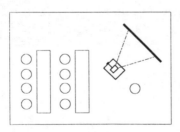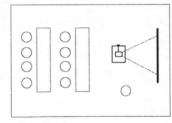

If the screen is placed at an angle to the audience they must look at you, or the screen, but not both. If the screen is placed centre stage, they can see the display and you at the same time. Assuming that you have designed your foils or slides correctly, they should be simple enough to focus the viewers' attention on what you are saying, thereby reinforcing it.

Incidentally, you may not have a choice about where the screen is positioned. Many presentation facilities have the screen in a fixed location (usually in the 'head on' position). If you are likely to be working at several different sites, it is worth practising with both set-ups so that you feel comfortable in either setting.

Please be seated

Having located your screen you now need to seat your audience.

A minor point of little interest? Not so! Seating arrangements can have a profound effect on the way that members of the audience respond to both the presenter and the presentation.

If it is up to you to arrange the seating at a presentation, you need to take account of two main factors:

- Audience size.
- Degree of interaction required between members of the audience and between the audience and the presenter.

The intimate brain storm

For small groups, and situations where you want the atmosphere to be reasonably open and a certain degree of discussion is expected, the correct seating arrangement will be the *round table* or the *open circle*:

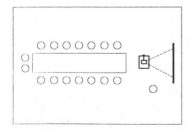

Round table layout

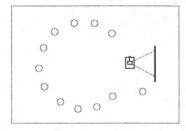

Open circle layout

The round table layout is appropriate if the audience will need a flat surface for drinks, to write notes, and so on. Where the main activity is to be a discussion, and will last for an hour or two at most, the open circle seating plan may be more effective in allowing communication between the participants.

Note. These seating plans are unsuitable for groups of more than 20 to 24, and work best with groups of 12 to 15 people.

Divided to conquer
Two of the most commonly used seating layouts for medium sized groups (say 20 to 30 people) are the *open square* and the *block*. They are easily adapted to fit wide rooms or narrow rooms and a variety of audience sizes with very little trouble:

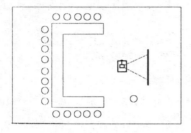
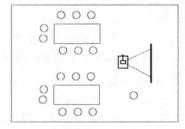

Open square layout   **Block layout**

These set-ups can be used for informal or formal presentations as well as training sessions and any type of group which involves a certain degree of discussion, but which does not require the relative intimacy of the round table or the open circle.

The main weakness of the open square is that it reinforces the position of the presenter as the focus of attention, thus doing very little to encourage any team feeling.

For situations where a sense of team membership is an integral part of the event, you may prefer to use the block seating plan. This seating arrangement creates individual groupings within the audience as a whole and thereby encourages a team feeling and a greater willingness to interact as a group rather than just as individuals.

The most significant setback associated with this seating order is the fact that the people seated along the inside edge of each block need to turn sideways on to the table in order to see the screen or flipchart. This might prove counter-productive if the audience is required to do a great deal of note-taking during the presentation, and in such cases the open square plan would be preferable.

Come one, come all
For larger audiences (30 and over) there are three basic styles of seating plan that are suitable: the *conference*, the *restaurant* and the *theatre*.

The main factors affecting your choice between these three plans are:

• How long is the event?
• Are the audience required to take notes, or merely sit, look and listen?
• How much room is available in relation to the size of the audience?

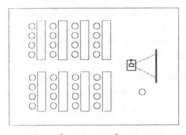

Conference layout

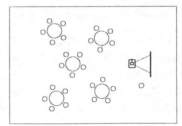

Restaurant layout

The conference layout allows a medium to high level of interaction between audience and presenter and is indicated where:

• The event will last at least one full day.
• The audience will need to take notes.
• Only low to medium interaction is required between members of the audience.
• Finding a large enough room to run the presentation with chairs and tables will not be a problem.

The restaurant style of seating is much favoured by some of the top business presenters, allowing a high level of interaction between the presenter and his audience (especially if the presenter uses the seating area as part of his own working space). It is often the only seating option where the presentation is being run in a hotel.

It is an arrangement which also favours high interaction between members of the audience, if required, and can serve to enhance team identity (at the table-by-table level). Unfortunately, however, this same group identification can mean trouble for a presenter who is not used to working in this kind of situation and group activities can easily spill over into the presentation sessions.

Generally speaking, this layout is really only indicated where:

- The event will *not* last for more than one full day.
- The audience will need to do very little note-taking.
- The presenter has well developed 'crowd control' abilities.

A further feature of this type of layout is the fact that it is inevitable that at least one or two people at each table (depending on the size of the tables) will need to spend most of their time facing towards the presentation area and away from the table. Many people find this arrangement somewhat unsettling and for that reason alone it is best avoided if possible. The only alternative is to have chairs round only the back half of the table – possibly an unacceptable waste of space where large numbers of people must be accommodated.

The last option – the theatre seating plan – is most suitable where:

- The event will last for no more than one full day.
- The audience will not need to take notes.
- Interaction between the audience and the presenter is not a key feature of the event.
- No room can be found which is large enough to accommodate a presentation with both chairs and tables.

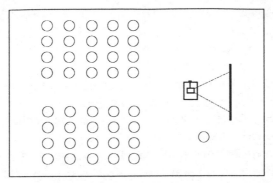

Theatre seating plan

This is another style of seating much favoured in hotel-based presentations. Unfortunately, hotel chairs are seldom of a sort designed for comfortable sitting over a prolonged period and this fact should be allowed for by providing correspondingly frequent comfort breaks.

If you want it done properly
One last word of warning before we leave the subject of seating arrangements:

- *Never* assume that hotel staff will automatically know how to prepare a room for a presentation.
- *Always* provide clear instructions in advance, preferably including a diagram of the required layout.
- *Always* check the room layout for yourself on the day of the event *in plenty of time for it to be put right, if necessary.*

So many switches – so few hands

Only experience will teach you all the precautions that you need to take when doing a presentation away from home. Listed below are some of the most important pointers to setting up an effective presentation:

- When using electrical equipment always start by checking the location of the power outlets. Provide your own 'gang plug' and an extension lead to avoid difficulties caused by badly placed power outlets.

- Is everything set up correctly? Have you checked *every* piece of electrical equipment?

  If you're using an OHP, check that the screen and projector are correctly angled in relation to each other (the front of the projector and the screen should be parallel). If the projected image is larger on one side of the screen then pull that side forwards (towards the projector) until both sides of the image are equal.

  Also, make sure that you have room to stack used and unused foils in separate, easy-to-reach piles. Experiment to find an arrangement that feels comfortable, bearing in mind the need to stay clear of the screen area when changing foils.

- Check the heating/air conditioning controls. How accurate are they? Can they be easily reset? (In older buildings it may be difficult to control the heating on a room-by-room basis.)

  Keep the room slightly cool, even when full of people, in order to keep the members of the audience from getting so comfortable that they start to doze off.

- If the room/hall is large enough to require a sound system, is the microphone set at the right height (or are you going to be using a wire-less microphone)? In either case, make sure that you do a proper sound check *before* the event.

  Few things are more unnerving than to start speaking and be interrupted by electronic feedback – the audible equivalent of sticking a knitting needle in one ear and out of the other. Feedback occurs when the output from one device (usually one of the speakers) is being picked up by the microphone, then sent back to the speaker, which feeds it to the microphone, and so on. (By the way, the signal from the speaker may not be loud enough to cause feedback until someone speaks into the microphone, so always do the soundcheck even if everything seems OK.)

- If someone else is turning lights on and off during your presentation, make sure you run a last-minute rehearsal. If necessary, run several rehearsals until both of you are sure that you understand what needs to be done.

  If the lighting causes intrusive reflections, can you turn

some lights off? If several lights are controlled by a single switch and you don't want to turn them all off, can you remove some of the bulbs to get the required result?
- Check the audience area. Are there any broken seats? Get rid of them. Are there any soiled table covers? Have them replaced. If you are providing notepads, pens, handouts, soft drinks or water, and so on, is everything correctly set out?
- Check your own area. Do you know what adjustments you will need to make (if any) after the previous speaker has finished?

  Do you have a carafe of water and a glass on hand (see Chapter 14)?

  If a lectern is provided, is it the right height? Does the light work (if any)?
- Use clearly visible tape to hold down, and clearly mark, any electric cables that could trip someone up.

The little things that count

Finally, having ensured that the presentation room is ready for business, there are just a few last little touches that will help to make your audience feel comfortable during the event:

- Where will tea and coffee be served *before* the presentation begins?

  Having the smell of good quality coffee wafting around is a well-known way of making a home more attractive to potential buyers. If you have the space, why not make the presentation room seem more welcoming by serving the first tea and coffee of the day at the back of the presentation room itself (make sure that it won't be cleared until the first mid-session break).
- Make sure that the staff responsible for clearing the crockery away won't interrupt the presentation. If possible, have refreshments served in another room.
- Now that smoking, and especially passive smoking, is a major social issue, you will need to designate specific smoking and non-smoking areas.

- Check the number of seats against the number of delegates. (If you aren't sure exactly how many seats are needed, put out as many seats as you think you will need, and have some spare chairs stacked away in a corner.)
- If you're working with fixed seating, and there are clearly more seats than delegates, rope off the back row(s) of the audience area, and put out some 'RESERVED' notices.

CHAPTER 13
Questions, Answers and Hecklers

Why?

Here are just three of the many good reasons why you might want to accept questions from your audience:

- To create positive interaction between the members of the audience and yourself.
- By accepting audience questions *during* a presentation any misunderstandings or confusion can be cleared up on the spot.
- The questions from the audience will give you a clearer idea of their level of understanding and special areas of interest, allowing you to fine tune your performance.

When?

If allowing questions at any time has advantages, it also has certain disadvantages from the presenter's point of view:

- You may get sidetracked by questions which are not strictly relevant.
- Questioners frequently ask about things that are of special concern to them as individuals.
- It is very easy to lose track of time while answering

questions so that you end up having to rush through the last part of the presentation, in order to end on time.

- An unexpected or awkward question may disrupt the flow of the presentation and leave you looking ill-informed and unprofessional.
- In a 'worst case' scenario the questions could take up so much time that you cannot complete the presentation.

Daunting as the disadvantages may appear, there are relatively simple strategies for avoiding each and every one of them, or at least of containing the negative effects.

Taking control of audience questions

One simple and very effective way of allowing questions while still keeping the presentation on track goes like this:

> 'I'll take any questions which call for *clarification* at any time during the presentation, but any questions which require *additional information*, or which relate to anything *not* directly covered in the presentation will be dealt with at the end of the session.'

This approach assures the audience that you will cover all questions before the event is over, and also gives you the option of answering each question or putting it on hold as you see fit.

The three basic secrets of handling questions

Secret No 1
It is a natural reaction to start working out the answer to a question while the questioner is still speaking. Unfortunately, it is impossible to give your full attention to two separate lines of thought at the same time.

So, while a questioner is speaking, *listen*. Cut a long-winded question short, by all means, but only start thinking about the answer *when the question is complete.*

Secret No 2

A common pitfall, when taking questions, arises when only the presenter, the questioner and the first few rows of the audience know what question the presenter is answering. Fortunately, there is a remarkably simple solution.

Except in one special case (which is covered on page 92) whenever you receive a question:

- *rephrase* the question and then *repeat* it to the whole audience *before* you answer it;
- then address your answer to the *whole* audience.

This action has three distinct advantages:

- If the questioner does not correct your rephrased version of the question, you can be reasonably sure that you have both heard the question and understood it.
- Everyone in the audience knows what is going on.
- You can think approximately five times faster than you can speak, so by repeating the question, you give yourself valuable extra time in which to think about your answer.

Secret No 3

Avoid the trap of allowing yourself to be monopolised by just a handful of questioners.

Having accepted and repeated a question, aim to regulate your eye contact in the ratio of 20 to 25 per cent to the questioner, 75 to 80 per cent to the rest of the audience.

Looking at someone as you finish speaking is an implied cue for a reply. Only look at the questioner as you finish your answer *if you actually want the dialogue to continue.* Then you might also reinforce the message by asking something like: 'Does that answer your question?'

To *avoid* a follow-on question, simply direct your gaze to some other part of the room as you finish speaking and indicate that you are ready to take a new questioner.

What to do when you don't know the answer

Be honest. Say 'I don't know' or, better still, 'I don't know, but I will find out'. An even better response would be: 'I don't know, but I will find out by the end of the lunch break/tomorrow morning/etc.' And when you *say* you'll get the answer, make sure that you do.

An excuse is a loaded gun

Making excuses – for being late, for losing your place, for not knowing an answer, or any other slip up – is a dangerous move. The excuse may be entirely true, but in the long run it solves nothing and excuses always tend to sound extremely feeble, even when they are true.

Dr Heckle

Dr Heckle 'questioners' don't really want to ask a question so much as make a provocative or disruptive statement. This is one time when you definitely *should not* repeat what has been put to you, even if the question/statement reflects to your benefit. Three easy actions will stop this kind of heckling:

- Ask the 'questioner' to identify herself. This breaks the audience's concentration, gives you extra time to prepare an answer, and starts to defuse the troublesome statement.
- Review the statement, looking for the underlying motive.
- Use your analysis of the statement to rephrase it as a question, and make the content less antagonistic.

For example, the 'statement':

I don't see how you expect to increase the sales of our patent widgets when 50 per cent of our output is returned within six months!

Can be reworded as:

OK, Joan has made a good point here – how can we improve our production standards so as to increase our sales?

You don't have to distort a statement in order to turn it into a question, and if someone makes a statement so loaded that you'd rather not deal with it at all, simply defer it thus:

> That's not really something I can give a straight 'yes' or 'no' answer to, but I'll be happy to discuss it with you in more detail when we break for coffee/lunch/tea.

Mr Jibe

A 'Mr Jibe' differs from a Dr Heckle by appearing to be siding with and assisting the presenter. Mr Jibe questions usually start: 'Isn't it true that ...?'

The problem here is the ambiguity. The question may be an attempt to show off, or a deliberate attempt to trap you into a mistake. It may even be a genuine question! So, always wait until *you* are sure of the facts before you give an answer.

Beware the 'early bird'

An 'early bird' is a character who simply cannot wait to get at the 'worm' — the part of the presentation that she is particularly interested in. If the worm doesn't appear in what she considers to be a reasonable time then she just has to get in there to try to rootle it out with a probing question.

The best way to deal with an early bird is to give her recognition and cut the question short all in one go, thus:

> I do plan to cover that topic a little later on. Let me jot your question down so that I don't forget to cover it when we get to the appropriate point.

This response reassures the questioner that her enquiry has been taken seriously and will be addressed.

Bones of contention

Some time or other you are bound to run into a 'hidden absolute' — a 'question' that starts with a phrase such as:

> Everyone knows that ...
> It's quite obvious that ...

To take the sting out of this kind of question: *act dumb and ask for validation*. Do this by concentrating on the question, not on the questioner. For example, let's suppose that Chris, a member of the audience, decides to question a course of action proposed by the presenter:

Chris: 'It must be obvious to everyone here that [this course of action] is bound to fail.'

Presenter: 'It has been suggested that the proposed action may not be completely successful. As proposer of the action I can't really agree with that idea. But what do other people think?'

'Would the people who *don't* agree with the proposal like to raise their hands.'

The hidden absolute here is in the word 'everyone', though what Chris was probably trying to imply was 'everyone except you (the presenter)'. And that's why a calm response is bound to win out. An absolute can only be true if it is *absolutely true*. Yet we already know that the presenter at least believes that the action will succeed, so the hidden absolute cannot be true.

The presenter could have set up a popularity contest by asking 'Who agrees with Chris?'. By taking a more gentle line he is able to:

- Rephrase the original statement as a suggestion.
- Demonstrate that the hidden absolute is incorrect, but without being confrontational.
- Turn the vote into a 'sounding out' exercise, thereby removing the emotional charge.
- Propose the vote in negative terms. Since most people dislike agreeing to a negative proposition, this will minimise the support for the original statement.

Alternatively, the presenter could have asked a question such as: 'I wonder what makes you think that?' (An abrupt 'Why do you say that?' is definitely *not* the right way to tackle this kind of situation.)

Don't be afraid to hand the floor over to the speaker for a

short while; and when you think they've said enough simply thank them politely for voicing their *opinion* and insist on moving on to the next question.

The good, the bad and the ugly

When you are adequately prepared, dealing with genuine questions should not present any serious problems. Even the odd 'difficult customer' can be handled using the following procedure:

Step 1. Relax
Your natural reaction to an unduly loud, contentious or rude 'question' from the audience will be to tense up, with throat dry and heart beating faster as extra adrenalin is pumped into your bloodstream. To counter these reactions allow yourself to withdraw mentally, saying to yourself: 'I am thinking about the fact that I feel threatened.'

The very act of thinking about your feelings will enable you to view the situation more calmly, and deal with it appropriately.

Step 2. Be firm and polite
No matter how bad the situation looks, be firm and polite. An audience will only support a presenter against a heckler as long as the presenter is *perceived* to be in control of himself.

Step 3. Check the audience's body language
This will be a valuable clue as to what to do next:

- If people are exchanging looks and settling back as though they know exactly what's coming next you are up against a regular heckler. See Step 4, Option 1.
- If people are paying more attention to the heckler than to you then they are probably in agreement with what is being said. See Step 4, Option 2.
- If people look irritated and are watching you rather than the heckler then they are probably waiting for you to resolve the situation. See Step 4, Option 1.

● When all else fails, see Step 4, Option 3.

Step 4 – Option 1

If you think the heckler is simply sounding off ask him what answer he would give. Remain calm and courteous until the heckler runs out of steam, or the other members of the audience begin to look bored, then bring the incident to a close with a brief acknowledgement such as:

> Well, you clearly have very strong views on this matter, but I think we've taken the matter about as far as we can for the moment and I'm afraid I'm going to have to move on ...

Maintain eye contact with the heckler for the first part of your response, but then make an obvious point of looking away – in search of further questions or comments – as you finish.

Step 4 – Option 2

When a questioner appears to have considerable support from other members of the audience you will need to make a tactical decision as to the consequences of continuing the discussion.

Above all, be honest. The audience may not like your answer if it turns out that you really cannot give the answer they want, but most people *can* see when they're being told the truth, and if you stand your ground in a reasonable manner then it is more than likely that you will carry the day.

Step 4 – Option 3

If nothing else works you may have to cut the heckler short. Make it clear that you feel that you have done as much as you can to satisfy the heckler's demands and can do no more.

If you have indeed played fair with the heckler, the other members of the audience will probably help to settle the matter for you through a show of mass disapproval.

CHAPTER 14
Personal Presentation

Here I stand

It is truly amazing how easy it is to become self-conscious about your body when you give your first few presentations. How should you stand or move, for example?

- No matter what you may have heard, moving around is no better, and no worse, than standing still.
- When standing still, aim to have your feet about shoulder width apart and keep your body square on to the audience, with your toes pointing slightly outwards. This stance is comfortable to maintain in a relaxed, self-assured manner.
- Make sure that you are clearly visible to your audience, especially when you are saying something important. If you stand in front of a bright light your audience won't see much more than a black shape (which will be received as a negative image).

Here are some important 'posture pointers':

- Settling in one spot, leaning to one side.
  Hidden message: 'I'm bored and I'd rather be somewhere else.'
  Solution: When standing still, keep your weight evenly balanced and your hips level.
- Leaning over the top of the lectern.
  Hidden message: 'I'm too tired to stand up straight – or I just can't be bothered to do so.'
  Solution: When using a lectern, stand to one side rather than behind it.

- Sitting on the table provided for your notes, the OHP, etc.
  Hidden message: 'I don't have to make an effort here, because I'm more important than you.'
  Solution: No matter how relaxed you feel, stay standing!

In short, there is no ideal stance. Within reason, do whatever feels right for *you*. It is far more important that your verbal content, vocal style and body language should be congruent (all giving the same message) than whether you walk ten feet or ten miles while delivering your presentation.

You've got to hand it to him

The best way to use your hands during a presentation is to act as though you were in a normal conversation. If you usually wave your hands around in an animated fashion, do the same thing (within reason) in a presentation. And if you don't usually make much use of your hands when you're talking, that's fine too.

In short, if it doesn't feel comfortable then don't do it – and don't worry about it either. The audience have no idea what to expect from you, and what they never see they won't miss.

Tip:
If it feels natural to use your hands when talking, make sure that your gestures during a presentation are appropriate for the size of audience. Thus, the *more people* you are talking to, the *bigger* your hand and arm movements will need to be.

It may help you to decide what to do with your hands if you rehearse in front of the mirror or a close friend.

Here are some poses you might want to avoid:

- The 'stand at ease' stance – feet firmly planted and hands clasped behind your back. This looks stiff and overly formal. It is an 'authoritarian' stance, and will make it much harder to establish any degree of rapport.

- Having your hands in your pockets looks overcasual, even sloppy. Having said that, if you find that your hands have wandered into your pockets:
  - Remove your hand(s) from your pocket(s) in a leisurely manner at a suitable moment (to point at something in a visual display, to turn a page of your notes, or whatever)
  - And for the men, if your hands find their way into your trouser pockets, then above all, keep them still. If you fiddle with something, no matter how innocent you may be, at least half of your audience are guaranteed to interpret your actions in the worst possible way!
- Clasping your hands in front of you in the 'fig leaf' position looks rigid and uncomfortable and is generally recognised as a *defensive* posture, particularly for men. This stance will tend to set you apart from your audience and will lower your esteem in their eyes. It won't do much for your own self-confidence either.
- Standing with your hands on your hips can look arrogant, affected or just plain silly, depending on your general physique.
- Folding your arms over your stomach or chest can appear domineering in a large person, and is otherwise recognised as a defensive or divisive posture.
- Rubbing your hands together in a 'washing' motion looks creepy, fussy and possibly dishonest.

Just one look

The most basic link between any two people is *eye contact*. It is important, then, that you maintain continuous eye contact with your audience. Two key elements which ensure dynamic eye contact with an audience are *timing*, and the *Aura Effect*.

As far as timing is concerned, you should look at any particular person for no more than three or four seconds. Shift your gaze frequently, and preferably randomly (it is quite distracting to see an inexperienced presenter sweeping her gaze back and forth across an audience like some kind of human searchlight).

It is not necessary to look at every single member of the audience in order to maintain effective contact. Indeed, the Aura Effect allows you to make effective contact as it works on the principle that our field of vision 'fans out' as it gets farther away:

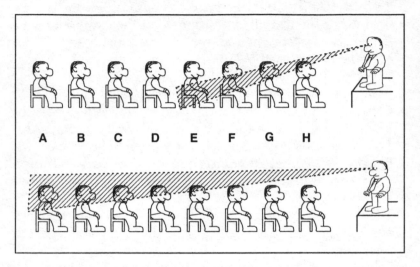

The Aura Effect extends to the sides, in front of and behind the person the presenter is actually looking at. Thus, in the illustration, the presenter makes direct eye contact with one person at the front of the audience, and at least four or five people will think he is looking straight at them. When the presenter turns his gaze towards the back of the audience, however, as many as 15 to 20 people are likely to believe that the presenter is looking at them, and them alone.

In general terms, you will want to maintain continuous eye contact with your audience. But there are times when it can actually be beneficial if you deliberately *break* eye contact.

If, for example, you ask your audience to think something through for a few moments, you will get a better response if you lead the way by breaking eye contact and then mime being thoughtful.

To sum up, the overall image that you need to project for the best effect is one of relaxed control. This impression is most easily produced if it reflects what you really feel – when you know that you've done everything you can to ensure that the presentation goes well.

Four keys to success

If this book were distilled into four key points they would be:

- **Know your audience**
  Who do you really need to talk to? What do you want them to hear? How do you want them to react? What will motivate them to respond in the desired manner?
- **Keep it simple**
  Language is an extremely inadequate medium for expressing any but the most simple ideas. So KISS (**K**eep **I**t **S**hort and **S**imple), and always talk to your audience as they are, not as you would like them to be.
- **Keep to the Point**
  Don't underestimate your audience – but don't over-estimate them, either. Be realistic. You only have a limited timeframe in which to tell your audience what they need to know, not everything that you know.
- **Have confidence in yourself and in your message**
  The audience will usually be on your side, at least at the start of a presentation. If you look confident and sound confident (but not arrogant) it is very probable that you will keep them on your side, even if you do make the odd mistake. You are far more likely to undermine that goodwill by being pompous or timid than by fluffing your lines, putting up the wrong slide or foil, or by running foul of the odd heckler.

Style of speaking

Given that we develop our way of speaking over many years, can we really hope to develop a whole new vocal style?

But why not? All it takes is that you should want to improve your verbal skills. And the word *improve* really is crucial in this respect. Think of this as a progressive process, as an extension of your abilities.

Practise in front of a mirror and by talking into a tape recorder or a video camera. It doesn't really matter *what* you say at this point so much as *how* you say it. Find ways to make your voice more interesting, more expressive and more authoritative. As the ultimate test, read a column from your local telephone directory so that it sounds interesting, amusing or persuasive. You'll be amazed at how quickly you can develop your vocal skills.

Taking care of your voice

The *Big Ben* exercise (also known as the *King Kong* routine) is an easy yet effective way of deepening your voice and enhancing its flexibility.

Make yourself comfortable, taking care that you are not constricting your chest or diaphragm in any way. Now, starting in your normal tone of voice, work your way down the scale singing 'ding, dong, bing, bong'. Keep going until you reach the lowest note that you can manage without straining your vocal cords. Then work your way up the scale until you reach the highest note that you can manage without strain. Finally, work your way back down the scale until you reach your normal tone of voice.

Repeat this exercise four or five times each session, one or two sessions per day, and you'll be amazed at the results. Your normal speaking voice will deepen; the range of notes that you can cover (without stress) will widen; and your voice will become more flexible, more varied and, above all, more interesting.

When you have acquired an interesting and flexible speaking voice, remember to keep it well exercised. During the colder months take care that your throat is well protected when you go outside, and always take the appropriate kind of throat tablets or medicine if you detect any sign of soreness or irritation.

Rehearsals

Your rehearsal(s) for a presentation should be part of the process of preparing your script.

Once you have drafted the outline of your script, put it on audio tape (video tape is even better) then run it through with the following thoughts in mind:

- Does your presentation follow a clear sequence of ideas?
- Have you aimed the material at the right level?
- Have you included material that isn't strictly relevant?
- Are you trying to cover too much information?
- How and where can you use visual aids to clarify and enhance the basic presentation?
- Are you presenting your material in an appropriate manner?

Armed with the answers to these questions, and any others which seem important to you, work your first draft into something more precise. When you think that you've developed a script that does what you want it to do, have another recorded rehearsal, asking yourself whether it really achieves the required result. It will also pay to take note of the *vocal interest* in your delivery (plus your *body language*, if you're doing a video recording).

When you first begin to give presentations you might also want to set the microphone a little way away from you so that you can learn to project your voice. There are two main points of difference between *projecting* your voice and *raising* your voice (technically referred to as shouting):

1a To project your voice you must use your *diaphragm* to drive the air up through your throat and mouth.

1b When you shout you use your *neck muscles* to do all the work.

2a When you project your voice, you should find that you can talk as easily as if you were conversing with someone only a matter of inches away. Projecting your voice should not cause any kind of physical strain.

2b When you shout, it *hurts!*

If you have trouble learning to project your voice correctly you may find that it is worth paying a couple of visits to a professional voice coach or singing teacher.

Finally, when you feel that you've got things almost right, stop rehearsing. To give a really good performance you must have as much interest in your presentation as you want to see in your audience, and that's not very likely if you've rehearsed it to death.

Night and day, you are the one

The best state to be in just before you give a presentation is relaxed but alert. This may depend on whether you are a 'day person' or a 'night person'.

Day people find it easy to make an early start, but they tend to run out of steam later in the day. Night people, by contrast, may find it quite hard going to handle early morning sessions, and will be far more lively in the afternoon. If you are a night person and you have to give a presentation in the early morning, set the alarm at least a half-hour early. This will give your body enough time to get into gear before you step into the spotlight.

For relaxation, on the other hand, you might like to consider listening to a tape of violin music by Mozart or one of the baroque composers (Vivaldi, Handel, etc), which is restful without causing drowsiness.

Limbering up

Muscular tension can also affect your ability to speak easily and clearly. It is a good policy, therefore, to do a little limbering up before you speak to get your body into the right state.

A little deep breathing is a good way to start. Make sure that you get plenty of oxygen into your bloodstream, but don't overdo it. Just three or four deep breaths will normally be sufficient to give you a bit of a lift. If you feel the least bit dizzy then stop immediately – you're probably hyperventilating and that won't help at all.

A safe way to loosen up your neck and shoulder muscles is known as the *Chicken Peck*.

Standing in a comfortable position, with your spine as straight as possible, slowly push your chin out so that your whole head moves forward – making sure that your chin does not drop. Then bring your head back as far as it will go, still keeping your chin at the original angle. Do this 10 or 12 times in a steady rhythm, being careful not to strain the neck muscles.

Desert mouth syndrome

Apart from forgetting what to say, nothing is worse than literally 'drying up' during a presentation.

The first part of the remedy is to avoid anything that could cause 'desert mouth syndrome'. This includes salted snacks (crisps, peanuts, etc), smoking, and stimulants such as alcoholic drinks, coffee, tea and carbonated soft drinks, all of which can irritate the throat and cause 'desert mouth syndrome'.

One of the most effective ways of stimulating the production of saliva is to suck on a slice of lemon or to drink a little lemon juice. A far more practical solution is to have a supply of chilled (but definitely not iced) mineral water mixed with a touch of lemon or lime juice (experiment to find a balance that suits your palate). This makes a truly refreshing drink and an infallible antidote to 'desert mouth'.

A 'mighty rushing wind'

And finally, make sure that you avoid anything which is likely to cause flatulence or hiccoughs. Here, again, carbonated drinks are among the major villains, not to mention spicy foods. Do bear in mind, as well, that both overeating *and* undereating can both cause embarrassing tummy rumbles during a presentation.

References

Argyle, M, Alkema F and Gilmour R (1970), 'The communication of friendly and hostile attitudes by verbal and non-verbal signals', *European Journal of Social Psychology*, Vol 1, pp 385–402.

Buzan, Tony (1989), *Use Your Head*, BBC Books, London (Revised edn).

Buzan, Tony (1989), *Use Your Memory*, BBC Books, London (Revised edn).

Honey, Peter and Mumford, Alan (1992), *The Manual of Learning Styles*, Peter Honey, Maidenhead (Revised edn).*

Honey, Peter and Mumford, Alan (1986), *Using Your Learning Styles*, Peter Honey, Maidenhead.*

Markham, Ursula (1989), *The Elements of Visualisation*, Element Books, Longmead.

Mehrabian, A and Ferris, R (1967), 'Inference of attitudes from nonverbal communication in two channels'. *The Journal of Counselling Psychology*, Vol 31, pp 248–52.

Miller, George A (1956), 'The magical seven, plus or minus two: some limits on our capacity for processing information', *Psychological Review*, No 63, pp 81–97.

O'Connor, Joseph and Seymour, John (1993), *Introducing Neuro-Linguistic Programming*, Aquarian/Thorson, London, (2nd revised edn).

Ostrander, Sheila and Schroeder, Lynn with Ostrander, Nancy (1981), *Super Learning*, Sphere Books, London.

Pease, Allan (1992), *Body Language*, Sheldon Press, London, (New edn).

Rose, Colin (1985), *Accelerated Learning*, Accelerated Learning Systems, Aylesbury.

*These books are published privately and are available directly from Peter Honey, Ardingly House, 10 Linden Avenue, Maidenhead, Berkshire, SL6 6HB, England.